To Strengthen Family Ties

TO STRENGTHEN
FAMILY TIES

LINDSAY R. CURTIS, M.D.

BOOKCRAFT INC.
SALT LAKE CITY, UTAH

Library of Congress Catalog Card Number: 74-84478
ISBN 0-88494-268-6

1st Printing, 1974

LITHOGRAPHED IN U.S.A.

PUBLISHERS PRESS
SALT LAKE CITY, UTAH

Contents

Preface

On the wall of my library hangs a coat of arms. Its commanding caption in Latin reads: *Fortis in Unitate Sunt. Curtis Fratres.* It pictures a bundle of sticks bound together by leather thongs. Behind this coat of arms lies a meaningful story, one that made an unforgettable impression upon my mind.

A family of twelve not only calls for hard work to make it go but also demands a lot of cooperative effort. This story of the bundle of sticks was vividly demonstrated more than once to our family of twelve as my mother taught us the importance of family ties.

Taking a small stick of wood, she easily snapped it in two.

"Now," she said, "let me show you what happens when I take a bundle of sticks and bind them together." With no amount of effort could she possibly break the bundle. The lesson was obvious to all.

"If you children will 'stick' together, you will give strength to each other. This strength can be a protection and a help to you all your life."

The Latin insignia says: "In Unity There Is Strength. Curtis Brothers."

Many have been the occasions during which we have depended upon this strength. Great has been the comfort of knowing such strength is behind us, supporting us at all times.

Any family can enjoy this strength—if they will strengthen their family ties. To such a noble purpose this book is humbly dedicated.

CHAPTER 1

Picking Priorities

The first disposable item that most of us can remember is the paper handkerchief. Since its advent, however, new disposables have been appearing in ever-increasing numbers.

For example, handtowels, washrags (even wet with a cleaning solution), diapers, tablecloths, eating utensils and thousands of other items have now become "disposable." They are used once, then thrown away.

Disposable hypodermic syringes and disposable transfusion sets are found in all hospitals. They are now used once, then thrown away. Needles and scalpel blades no longer have to be sharpened; like hundreds of other items used in medical care, they are used only once, then disposed of.

A fountain pen once was bought for "lifetime" use and guaranteed as such. Now it is cheaper to buy a new ballpoint pen from an automatic dispenser than it is to buy a bottle of ink.

More and more people are buying a new car, not with the idea of its lasting for many years, but with the thought of trading it in on a new one after a year or two.

It is possible in many cases that quality is being "traded in" for "expediency" and "convenience"! It's a changing world.

There are many things in life, however, which are not disposable and which never change. The lessons which the Savior taught two thousand years ago, for example, are just as bright and shiny and new today as they were then.

Likewise family ties are not disposable. The value of the love I feel for my family is greater than any earthly treasure, and what may be just as important, it grows stronger with age. We hope it will be eternal.

A wise, priority-minded philosopher once said, "Spend your life working for something that will outlast it." Family ties can be eternal, if we want them to be. They are worth strengthening because they will outlast this life.

A friend of mine complained, "I am not leaving much to my children." Another friend answered him, "You are leaving *everything* to them, including your good name, because you will be able to take nothing with you when you go!" The first man began to re-examine his list of priorities. He could leave to his children only the loving relationship he had with them.

President David O. McKay's most famous and oft-quoted maxim was, "No other success can compensate for failure in the home." Undoubtedly many have come to re-examine their priorities as a result of this wisdom.

A young man came to my office recently whom I had not seen for some time. For several months he had been working for his company in the home office located in a large city in the Eastern United States. "Why did you come back home?" I asked.

"It's a matter of priorities," he said. "I was offered a substantial raise and an exciting promotion, but I turned it down."

"Why?" I asked again.

"I'll give you the same reasons I gave my boss. There are three things terribly important in my life," he said, "my family, my God and my job, in that order. I felt that I could not keep them in that order of priority if I stayed in that city in that special situation and in that particular environment, so I came back home. I have not been sorry." Here was truly a priority-minded young man.

A few years ago I flew to the Midwest to attend a son's graduation. Following graduation, I was invited by my son to travel out West with him and his family by car. In spite of the inconvenience and crowding I might cause, my son was insistent. As a result of the extra passenger, however, he was forced to strap a cumbersome carrier on top of the car, into which he very carefully packed all of their treasures to make the trip back home. When this task stretched into a couple of hours, I inquired into the delay. "I am sorting everything carefully to avoid too much weight (in the carrier) on top of the car, Dad," he said.

"Why all the worry?" I volunteered. "Looks pretty compact to me."

"I'll show you later why I am concerned," he said. We dropped the subject for the moment and were soon on our way.

The next day as we approached the windy prairies of the Midwest my son said, "We'll soon reach the place about which I was worried, Dad, and then I'll show you *why* I was worried."

Shortly we approached a swale in the highway, on either side of which was littered with debris from overturned trailers and other wind damage. As our car with its heavy topload began to sway precariously, my son remarked, "This is the reason I was careful to avoid a top-heavy load, Dad. This is called 'Trailer-over Gulch.' As you can see, many vehicles have not made it through this area without tipping over."

Many of us allow our lives to become top-heavy with insignificant things. We lose track of our priorities. As the novelist Edith Wharton so aptly phrased it, "Lots of people get themselves into the thick of thin things."

"Accumulatus Morus" is a disease which is not found in the ordinary medical books. Its cause is obscure but it may be related to one's background and early environment.

The primary symptom of this disease is the desire to accumulate money, property, status or honor. The afflicted person may be one who has experienced poverty and hardship in childhood; or one who feels generally insecure in life.

Such a person begins with modest goals, which he achieves with great zeal, determination, and hard work. However, instead of being delighted with such an achievement, he is dissatisfied. Almost immediately he has set higher and higher goals, usually of a financial nature.

Because of the patient's eagerness to succeed and accumulate, he sometimes forgets about other people and their feelings. He may even trample unconcernedly on their God-given rights. His success brings with it great confidence but almost inevitably it also brings great pride.

Slowly and insidiously, Accumulatus Morus burrows into the patient's soul, too often striking on its greedy way that part of a man's brain which commands his sense of values. He develops a selective type of spiritual blindness.

His vision of true spiritual and moral values becomes dimmed, while his desire for temporal and material things becomes acute and almost compulsive.

The more he accumulates, the more he desires to accumulate and the less satisfied he becomes with what he has. He loses that feeling of serenity that comes with selfless service. Gradually he develops the hang-ups of the harassed. Soon he has traded the peace of mind of the compassionate for the guilt-filled, selfish, egocentric state of mind of the money-changer.

The cure for this malady is not to be found in medical books. This canker of the soul is not to be cured with wonder drugs. The cure was given by the Master Physician two thousand years ago. It reads: "For whosoever will save his life shall lose it, and whosoever will lose his life for my sake shall find it. For what is a man profited, if he should gain the whole world, and lose his own soul? or what shall a man give in exchange for his soul?" (Matthew 16:25-26.) Surely the Lord was talking on the subject of "Picking Priorities" for our lives.

We must be careful that this insidious disease, Accumulatus Morus, does not cause us to lose our sense of priorities.

Our first priority is the companion the Lord has given us as a wife or husband. The second is our children, and the third is our God, through His Church. All three are important, but their *place* in our list of priorities may be just as important.

Another sage, priority-oriented philosopher summed it up rather sensibly when he said: "Keep your eyes upon the Lord. Keep your heart turned to your wife. Keep your arms around your children." These are our priorities.

A family with strong ties knows its priorities!

CHAPTER 2

Take Time

Where the expression "time on our hands" originated I don't know. Perhaps this saying became obvious because time goes faster if we have something to keep our hands busy.

But time really rests on our minds. If our minds are busy, it doesn't seem to matter too much what we are doing with our hands. Isn't it strange that some people are burdened with so much time that it literally drags? They become bored and restless. Others, by contrast, can't possibly squeeze into the day all they have set for themselves to do.

A prisoner sitting out a life sentence looks at time from a different point of view than a man pushing to catch a plane. Yet from the time we are born, the Lord gives each of us the same twenty-four hours in every day.

Life may be compared to a suitcase which we must pack and unpack each day. Some people depend upon cramming things in as tightly as possible. Others pack in a methodical, orderly fashion, placing emphasis upon neatness. Some arrange things carefully to avoid wrinkling. Still others throw everything together in a haphazard, last-minute, on-the-run manner, leaving those things to hang out that can't be completely stuffed in.

Some are not selective as to what they take with them. Many unnecessary and worthless articles are too often included, leaving more valuable and useful articles behind. But to each of us is generally left the task of selecting *how* and with what our twenty-four-hour suitcase is to be packed.

It's true that great demands are made upon some of us. At times we wonder how we can possibly complete all the tasks assigned to us. Even church assignments can become overwhelming.

But a thoughtful review of our priorities combined with a meticulous rearrangement of our suitcase will allow us to complete the important tasks — with sufficient time left over to spend with our families.

Yes, the Lord has given everyone the same-sized suitcase in life, twenty-four hours a day. But it's our responsibility to determine how it shall be packed.

Dr. Russell Nelson, a busy and capable cardiac surgeon, not only carries on a demanding practice of medicine but also finds time to serve the Lord as President of the Sunday Schools of the Church. When his wife was asked how he fared as the father of ten children, in view of the demands made of him by his practice and his Church, she said, "When Russell is here he is *really here.*"

What she meant was that when he was with his family, his mind was not somewhere else. The time he spent with his family was quality time, devoted entirely to their interests.

To enjoy quality time with our family we must leave our problems at the office. When we close the door to our office, let's close our minds to our business problems.

In this ecology-oriented culture of ours, time is the one thing that cannot be recycled. Once it is spent it can never be recaptured. Its memories can, perhaps, but time itself cannot be recalled.

A busy bishop I know discontinued all interviews during Sunday School time. Instead he recognized this as one of the few opportunities he had to sit by his wife in church as they learned the gospel together.

An elders quorum president had previously gone home after priesthood meeting to watch television. As he reviewed his time-priority program, he decided to take his family to Sunday School where they would learn the gospel together.

A physician who was daily besieged by wall-to-wall patients placed his own wife's name on his appointment book, taking time out of his busy schedule to phone and visit with her — and tell her how much he loved her.

Those who intend to spend time with their families "later, when I am released from this calling," or "when I have the house paid for," or "when I can quit one of my jobs," or "when I am through as president of the service club," may awaken some day to find that life has passed them by, as have their families. "He who is always busy as a bee, may come home to find his honey gone."

A long time ago the government learned the value of the "pay-as-you-go" system, which establishes a priority for our money. Human nature being what it is, most of us would put off to the very last minute the payment of our taxes, only to find ourselves with insufficient money left to pay them. By deducting a pre-calculated amount out of each paycheck, the government not only takes care of its own interests but also eases the taxpayer's method of payment by forcing him to meet his obligations out of each check while he has the money in hand.

Our obligations to our family are just as important and certainly much more urgent than paying taxes. We might even be able to make up for taxes that are in arrears. But as stated, "time cannot be recycled"; we can't make up for time with our family that is in arrears.

No one forces us to spend a pre-calculated amount of time out of each week with our family. It is left to each of us to decide. But a pay-as-you-go program for spending time with our families might be desirable.

My wife and I toured part of Los Angeles after a forest fire had destroyed many lovely homes. From nearby forested areas to their rooftops the wind had carried treacherous sparks. Some homes had burned almost to the ground, while others standing next door had little more than a few scorched areas on the roof or had suffered no damage at all.

Our guide had a logical explanation. It seems that, when the threat of fire began, some people panicked and simply picked up what they could carry and fled the scene. Others stayed with their homes, busily watering down the roof and dowsing any sparks the instant they lit on their rooftops. Obviously their wearisome vigil paid off by saving their homes and belongings.

The time spent with our children may well serve the same purpose. When sparks of doubt and disbelief are flying about and threaten to engulf their children and their home, parents need to be around to water things down and to see that the flame doesn't get out of control.

Someone has said that we don't have to worry so much about guided missiles as long as we don't have misguided parents on the job. Admittedly we can't be present every minute, but we ought to be there when our children need us.

It must have been a great thinker who said: "It's better to set our sights on the stars and drag our feet in the treetops, than to aim for the treetops and drag our feet in the mud."

Let's spend all the quality time we can with our families. It will strengthen our family ties.

One of the most valuable efforts in this direction is the family home evening, an evening during which our family and our time with them receives top priority. Let's spend this evening each week with our families now while we have it instead of waiting until it is too late and time runs out.

The best thing to spend on children is time, and good intentions are a poor substitute for the time we might have enjoyed with our children and spouse. Note the following ode to good intentions:

I intend

> To talk less and listen more,
> To listen intently and understand more,
> To comment less and absorb more,
> To criticize less and empathize more.

I intend

> To suggest less and to help more,
> To judge slowly and ponder longer,
> To prod less and to compliment more,
> Yes, to intend less, but to do more.

—Lindsay R. Curtis, *Ensign,* June 1972

The road to hell may be paved with good intentions, but the road to heaven is so seldom traveled that paving doesn't seem necessary.

Two friends of mine have cabins close to one another in one of the nearby canyons. Both are horse-lovers and each owns horses, but there the similarity ends. One friend spends considerable time with his horses. He no sooner appears on the scene than his horses come running. They love to be petted, and they even love to be ridden by him. They recognize both his whistle and his voice immediately and run to his side.

By contrast, the other friend rarely has time for his horses. On the rare occasions when he does attend them, they ignore him. In fact, they run from him. Even oats and other enticements fail to bring his horses in spite of his pleading. After chasing after his horses almost to the point of his complete physical exhaustion the other day, he finally borrowed a horse in order to capture one of his own horses to ride.

We cannot expect our children to come at our beck and call when we seldom call or when our contact with them is infrequent.

Of the Good Shepherd we read: "And the sheep follow him: for they know his voice. And a stranger they will not follow, but will flee from him: for they know not the voice of strangers." (John 10:4-5.)

Our children should have the opportunity to know us well. And the time we spend with them should be a joyous occasion. They will then remember the good times they have had with us, the wisdom they may have learned from us, and they will enjoy the anticipation of future encounters with us. Certainly they will recognize our voice when we call them.

Yes, time is not only the best thing to spend on children, it is probably the best investment we can make in our family to strengthen its ties.

CHAPTER 3

Unity Begins with You Two

As a lifetime city dweller I was intrigued the other day to see the way two horses were standing in a field next to each other. Human beings would have been standing with their heads together discussing something or other. But not these horses.

At first I wondered why they stood head-to-tail alongside each other. I wondered if they were angry and were not speaking to each other in whatever language horses speak. Could they even be ignoring one another? Then I noticed that the day was warm and the numerous flies were bothersome — and that the horses were simply practical. They were actually looking out for each other.

As their tails kept active it became apparent that they were busily keeping the flies off each other. They were thinking in terms of "we" instead of "I." Truly many of the problems of marriage could be avoided if couples always thought in terms of "we" instead of "I."

Although the marriage comes first, it must still be in terms of a *relationship,* not forgetting one or the other as individuals. An unthinking husband remarked to his wife, "I think of you first as my wife." She wisely said: "Think of me first as a person."

Husband and wife must be united in purpose and effort if they are to be a support to their family. A discerning child soon discovers that he can drive a wedge between parents who are not united. He quickly learns to play one against the other, with the result that the husband-wife relationship is weakened and discipline of the child may be deficient.

The other day I had occasion to tear out some steps leading to my cabin in the hills. They were to be replaced with a small deck and some new steps. To my surprise, I found there, under the old steps, one-half of a pair of pliers, a half that I had lost many years ago shortly after the steps had first been built.

The half of pliers was now rusty and totally worthless. Likewise, the other half (that was not lost at first) had long since been misplaced, because it too was worthless without its partner.

I remember now when the pliers were new. They were shiny. They were chrome-plated. They had been an expensive, well-tooled, evenly matched pair. Securely fastening the two halves together were a nut and bolt. Carefully oiled, how well they functioned, and how many uses I found for that pair of pliers! But somehow the nut became loose, and instead of taking time to tighten the nut on the bolt to keep the two halves together I continued to use the pliers.

Not only did the "loose" pair of pliers become less efficient, but finally the nut fell off and was lost. Shortly thereafter one half of the pliers was also lost, apparently dropped between the boards on the steps. The two separate halves became totally worthless without each other.

Hopefully, this analogy will not be misunderstood, since there are circumstances over which we have no control; circumstances that may separate husband and wife. But the analogy is intended to point up the importance of each partner in a marriage relationship and how well the two can function together.

But their relationship must be secure. Just as the nut-bolt relationship on the pliers must be secure so that they may function well, so must the husband-wife relationship be one secured by a strong bond of love.

The best way for a husband and wife to teach unity to their family is to *be united* in purpose and in love. One of the most vulnerable places for Satan to strike is at the husband-wife unity. He has his foot in the door if he can cause a rift between husband and wife.

Mamie Eisenhower was asked how much she missed President Eisenhower. She said, "Yes, of course I miss him, but I don't grieve. We enjoyed nearly every pleasurable thing in life *together*. Occasionally I ask my son to let me put my head on his shoulder and to put his arm around me just to feel that strength once more which I felt with Ike." A true example of unity and a strong family tie.

Let me share with you a tender experience that so beautifully exemplifies unity in marriage.

The night was cold, damp, and forbidding in every sense of the word. It was the kind of night that a physician ordinarily would want to forget. Yet it was a night that I shall ever remember.

At age ninety-four my father had lived a full, useful, and successful life as the loving, tender, and considerate husband of his childhood sweetheart and as the overindulgent father of ten devoted children. Three months previously he had suffered a stroke that deprived him of the use of his legs and temporarily halted his speech.

Although the strength in his legs seemed gone forever, he gradually regained a partial, halting ability to talk. In spite of his advanced age, all of his numerous progeny had hoped and prayed for a return to the vigorous state of health in which we had always known him.

As the only member of the medical profession within our sizable family, I had brought him a considerable distance from his home town to the hospital in which I practiced so that I could be near him and watch over him with greater care. However, it now became apparent that our dad would never return to his home again. After three months of tender nursing, his once-vigorous body told us that it had served him

long and well but that it was now incapable of mending itself.
It had earned the right to be laid to rest.

In the middle of the night Dad's pulse weakened to almost imperceptibility. His temperature dropped below normal. His blood pressure faltered and slowly fell. Reflexes denoted the ebbing of life as they disappeared one by one. After three months of desperate fighting, his gallant spirit found its body no longer able to respond. Our dad was dying.

My first thought was that I should not bother my mother, whose state of health, at best, was precarious. She should not have her rest interrupted nor should she be brought out into the cold night on a forty-mile journey when she might be too late anyway. And if she did arrive before my father died she would find him in a coma from which he could not be aroused and in a terminal condition about which we as doctors could do nothing.

But then it occurred to me that sixty-six years of married life together had earned each of them the right to hold hands and hearts at the last moment of life on this earth. Surely this was a sacred right that was more important than any earthly reasoning that I might entertain. Neither Mother nor Dad would forgive me should I deny them this privilege.

Only with great effort did my mother make the journey to the hospital. In tender haste she was wheeled to the bedside of her comatose and dying companion. As was her custom when something was important, she had to stand up. She was literally lifted out of the wheelchair and onto her feet. Unsteadily she leaned over the blanched face of Dad, tenderly stroking the few gray hairs on his head as she had done thousands of times before.

Dad's last years were saddened by a gradual loss of hearing— but he always heard my mother when she spoke to him! There were no tears, no sobbing by Mother. She merely leaned over his head, kissed him softly, then spoke directly into his ear: "Oh, Father, I love you!"

Then something wonderful happened to this dying man. Suddenly yet slowly, a tear welled up in the corner of his eye. Even as the tear rolled down his cheek, his pulse quickened. His blood pressure began to rise and his reflexes slowly returned. Almost undetectable at first, but finally undeniably, Father began to rouse from his coma.

We left the room — except for Mother.

When we returned Father had lapsed back into his coma. But Mother said: "We had the grandest visit about some very important things."

You don't have to be a physician to know that the only thing on earth powerful enough to bridge the gulf between life and death is LOVE!

Father and mother, husband and wife, are granted a unique privilege on earth for a unity that isn't found in any other relationship. But it is a unity that is not bestowed upon couples without their seeking it themselves. It is a relationship that truly must be earned over the period of a lifetime.

A teenage boy, in a thoughtless moment of disrespect, used disgraceful language as he berated his mother over an inconsequential matter. Naturally this was later recounted to the boy's father.

The father was at first angered that his son would so disrespectfully and shamefully address his mother. But instead of remonstrating with his son in the same language the son had used to insult his mother, the father asked the boy if he might talk to him in private. The son was certain he would be chastised (probably physically) because his father loved his mother so deeply and tenderly. And he was fully aware of the great bond of respect between his parents.

When the son and father had retired to complete privacy, the father began to tell the son of his tender concern for the boy's mother. He also told the boy of his great love for him. As he did so he choked back the tears. He then asked his son if they might pray together.

As they knelt with arms around one another, the father began to pray, but soon found himself unable to say anything more. All the boy heard were sobs as he felt his father's arm

The son *knew* and felt at this moment the great love the father had for both of them. Nothing more had to be said. Needless to say, the incident of disrespect never recurred. Tearfully the son told his mother how much he loved her and apologized for his disrespectful behavior.

Unity in love can overcome almost any obstacle. And strong family ties begin with parents who are united.

CHAPTER 4

Children in the Family

Tessie Jones sobbed visibly and loudly, "I just can't live without Patti. After all, what is a home without children?"

The occasion for this outburst was the announcement two hours earlier by Tessie's youngest child, Patti, that she and Ron were to be married.

Tessie, age fifty-seven, and her husband Jim had successfully reared eight children and were now about to launch their youngest child via temple marriage. Ron was a young man of the highest caliber, truly worthy of his sweetheart, their daughter Patti.

"But what about Jim?" Tessie's friend Beverly started to say, "You and he can now . . ."

But Tessie interrupted her, "Jim? Jim has always been around. That's not the same as a son or a daughter."

When Tessie sobbed, "What am I going to do?" I was tempted to suggest, "Why don't you try being married?" It is significant that God officiated personally at the first wedding of mankind, and impressed the first couple with the importance of their relationship when He said: "Therefore shall a man leave his father and his mother, and shall cleave unto his wife: and they shall be one flesh." (Genesis 2:24.)

First comes the eternal relationship of husband and wife. Out of this union come children. But these children will eventually leave their father and mother to form an eternal relationship of their own with a spouse of their choice.

Children are a blessing. And certainly children that are entrusted into our care, children that are permitted to be born into our family and into our stewardship should be loved and tenderly cared for and taught. But it was never intended that love should be transferred from the spouse to the children.

Each of us should love our spouse above all others. But there is adequate love so that neither spouse nor children should be lacking in that important relationship. Unfortunately Tessie, in developing love for her children, had lost the intimate unity and the strong bond of affection that she should have had for her husband.

Marriage is a partnership ordained of God, one in which a man and a woman enter into a relationship in which they covenant to love and sustain one another. "Neither is the man without the woman, neither the woman without the man, in the Lord" (1 Corinthians 11:11); and could we add, "regardless of children"?

When this marriage is solemnized through the Holy Priesthood, God automatically becomes a member of this marriage partnership.

One of the principle objectives of this marriage union is to become partners with God in the creation of an eternal family. But husband and wife must be united as one if they are to effectively teach their children gospel principles and rear them in righteousness. Just like a team of horses, they must pull in the same direction if the load is to get anywhere. In many instances the progress of the children will be proportionate to the unity of the parents.

The number of children a couple should have and when they should have them is a matter that is strictly between them and the Lord. We are commanded to multiply and replenish the earth. At this point, however, the Lord leaves it up to us. He leaves it to our judgment to decide when or how many children we should have.

It is unfair for us to judge our neighbors by our personal opinions when it comes to family size. We don't know their circumstances. We don't know their problems or their particular situation, hence we cannot pass judgment as to how many children they should have. There may be extenuating circumstances (strictly the private and intimate domain of the couple concerned) that dictate the size of the family they will have.

However, men should be considerate of their wives who bear the greater responsibility not only of bearing children but of caring for them through childhood. The mother's strength should be conserved and the husband's consideration for his wife is his first duty.

A husband and wife should exercise wisdom and discretion in solving all marital problems. Prayerful consideration will direct them in making these important decisions, including those concerned with bringing children into the home.

A husband who neglects his relationship as well as his commitment to his spouse, while pursuing other interests (sports, hobbies, business, even church), will not be held blameless. Neither, however, is a wife without blame who transfers her complete love and attention and time to her children, while neglecting the partner she has covenanted to love and to cherish.

Lila is a mother of seven children. To the best of her ability she is a good mother. But Lila is a poor organizer. Seven children simply overwhelm her. She is never caught up with her housework. Because of fatigue she becomes impatient with the children.

On two occasions she has been hospitalized with a nervous breakdown. On one occasion, when her nerves were frayed and her patience had run out, a friend happened by just as she was battering their youngest child. By now her nerves were so far gone that she did not realize what she was doing.

ferred further children altogether.

But Bryant is unhappy with the decision of the bishop. He feels they should and will have more children — now! Bryant has lost sight of their relationship. He is thinking of himself rather than of Lila and her health. He is failing to think of her as a person.

The Lord has not set a limit on the number of children we should be allowed to have, nor has he set a minimum number that we are required to have. Remember, parents, children are a blessing, not an unwelcome obligation.

He has left it up to our own wisdom to decide how many children we want, and how many children we can care for. But He does hold us responsible for teaching them in His ways as well as we can. And I can't think of a better way to strengthen family ties!

CHAPTER 5

Loving the Unlovable

Someone has said that a person, particularly a teenager, has the greatest need to be loved when he is the least lovable.

Some of the most beautiful rocks may lie alongside the stream, their beauty temporarily obscured by mud. Any attempts to uncover them may be prevented by their sharp, jagged edges. Yet when these same rocks are dropped into the middle of a gushing mountain stream, the spilling, spurting waters quickly wash away the mud. As the rocks are tumbled and rolled, their sharp edges begin to be rounded off and the interesting and attractive underlying beauty is uncovered. At times all of this turbulence appears to be harsh and inconsiderate, but such refining and polishing is necessary to bring out the stone's inner loveliness.

The same sometimes applies to a child. Defensively he may have developed sharp edges on his personality. He may protect his inner, frightened self by masking his insecurity with the "mud" of unsavory language.

Too often he is unable to rid himself of the mud or the sharp edges by himself. As a result he is subjected to a painful, harsh process by which society washes and polishes him. In this often-abrasive process, the understanding love of a patient parent is what pumice is to polishing. Such a parent can bring out the luster from the depth of the child's soul. In fact, the family tie may be the tether to which he can attach himself.

air, by compression and cooling, lowering the temperature of air, it eventually became liquefied and could be changed from one substance to another.

He had brought some of this strange, ultra-cold liquid

air with him and proceeded to show what it could do to various articles. For instance, he quickly converted liquid mercury into a hammer head by freezing it with the liquid air and then used it to drive nails into a piece of wood. Allowing this same hammer head to stand at room temperature soon melted it into a liquid that could be poured from one container to another.

A bouncing rubber ball, after being dipped momentarily in the liquid air, shattered like a light bulb as it was again bounced against the hard floor.

By exposure to the liquid air a coil of soft lead was easily converted into an effective spring just as if it were fine-tempered steel.

It was an excellent demonstration of what happens when an environment is changed. It proved that physical properties of various substances can be altered radically by changing the environment.

So it is with our young people. Often by simply changing their environment we can change their properties, their ideals and their standards. An unloved child in an unloving environment may develop many undesirable qualities. But this same child, placed in a loving home, soon develops a feeling of security. He may ultimately discard his feelings of distrust and cynicism, replacing these with confidence and a sense of belonging.

A child who has been subjected to a constant negative attitude toward Christianity, toward Christian leaders, toward his church, and even toward all adults, when placed in the proper environment may change all of these attitudes. He may ultimately come to love Christ and His teachings and those who stand for such principles.

Objects react rapidly to exposure to liquid air. Human beings probably react more slowly to a new environment. But the results in human souls, though slower to take effect, ultimately may be much more profound than with inanimate objects; and the catalyst in this reaction may be the love the person feels as a result of his family ties.

One troubled young man who had been showered with most of the temporal things of life was asked what he desired more than anything else in the world. Whereas someone else his age might have answered, "Money, or diamonds, or a motorbike, or a car," this young man had a very different answer.

He said, "I would just like my dad to be more interested in me." He wanted and needed stronger family ties.

Those of us who are always "too busy" may well ponder this scripture: "For where your treasure is, there will your heart be also." (Matthew 6:21.)

We make time for the things we love to do. We allow unlimited time for the people we love. Sometimes we have to force ourselves to budget a few seconds for the unlovable.

Time and love are very much a part of our environment. The child who provokes us most may be just signaling us that he desperately needs help. The child who is the most unlovable probably has the greatest need for our love as part of his environment.

Sometimes our children are like rivers that absorb and pick up particles of material from the river bed over which they have flowed. As they do so, they become discolored and unattractive. For instance, there is a river in Algeria which picks up iron and gallic acid, two of the ingredients in black ink, as it winds its tortuous way through ore-filled mountains.

As one might expect, this river gradually becomes black as ink and is appropriately called the Black River.

In Southern Spain is found the Rio Tinto River or Colored River. This stream starts out in the hills near King Solomon's Mines as an emerald green color. As it flows through out-

This same water then slowly filters over a sandy stretch, sometimes temporarily trapped behind sandbars where it still is becomes red in color due to the oxidation process of the iron it contains. Almost reluctantly this same water turns to blood-red by the time it reaches the sea. It's small wonder that it earns the title of Rio Tinto or Colored River.

But this same water can also gradually free itself of the discolored sediment. It could race like a mountain stream over solid rocks, churning, aerating, and purifying itself as it goes, and eventually become crystal clear as it leaves all impurity behind.

So it is in life that man absorbs part of his environment, however brief the contact. It is difficult for our children to rub shoulders with either sin or righteousness without having some of it rub off on them. To a limited extent all of us are made up of small amounts of that with which we come in contact.

But by the same token our children cannot continually be in contact with greatness without becoming just a little greater themselves. They cannot come in contact with love without becoming more lovable. They cannot rub shoulders with honor without becoming more honorable. They cannot feel the touch of true compassion without becoming more compassionate.

Many a self-made great man has become great not only because of the hardships he had to overcome but also because of the great men and women who influenced his life along the way, not the least of which may be his parents. Colored rivers may be unattractive and unpleasant to behold but they still contain water capable of purification. Likewise our children are never lost nor have they reached the point where they cannot be purified and become godlike, especially if we will help them.

Anyone who has not experienced the heart-piercing anguish of a wayward child may have been spared suffering, but he may also have missed one of the Lord's greatest and most humbling lessons. May I relate here an experience that offers a meaningful analogy.

In this case it was only a shed I was building, but to me it was important. It was my self-assigned project.

Only two more boards and my task would be completed. To my chagrin, however, I fingered around in the sack and discovered I was out of nails. Hurriedly I looked around to see if I had dropped a few nails on the ground, and I had — but not enough to complete the shed and have it ready for painting.

We were in the mountains a considerable distance from any store. A special trip would have been inconvenient and costly.

After exhausting every source of supply and looking in every corner for straight nails, the thought suddenly dawned on me. What about the bent nails that I had thrown away? Could they be straightened? Could they still be used somehow to complete the shed?

Now I'm glad I ran out of nails. I'm grateful now that I had to straighten out those few nails and use them, for in doing so I learned a valuable lesson: "It's impossible to use a bent nail if you keep hitting it on the head."

But if you take this same nail and hold it in your hand and study it carefully, you soon learn where its weak spot is. You know where it was bent out of shape. Then you can lay it on its side and gently tap it in the right place and, lo! you've straightened it out.

If you then hammer it cautiously, not too hard, but firmly and squarely on its head, it becomes useful again. It develops "worth" again.

But I learned something else. A bent nail that has been straightened may give greater strength and hold the board more firmly than a new, straight nail, once it is in the wood. A "straightened" nail is not likely to come loose. And strangely

When they rebel we tend to reject them and almost cast them aside because they won't conform. And too often we try to force them to conform by continuing to hit them on the head.

But we need to stop hammering long enough to look at the problem. If we simply sit down with our young folks long enough to communicate with them and listen to *their* side of the question, we might begin to understand them.

With a gentle, friendly, understanding arm around their shoulder, we usually find that they and their problem can be straightened out without too much difficulty.

What a joy when we discover that, handled properly, the "bent-out-of-shapes" can be straightened out; they can become useful again! Instead of being quickly discarded like a bent nail and lost forever to society and to those who love them, they become more precious because of what they have been through.

Gentleness, compassion and understanding has salvaged these priceless souls. And how strong they have become and how firmly they hold in place — when they have found their "niche"!

Anyone can use a straight nail. It takes a wise and understanding carpenter to salvage a nail that is bent out of shape.

The other day I was holding my grandson on my lap. Soon he was exploring with his finger, first my nose, then my ear, my hair, and even my chin. How different I must look to him as he studies me from "down under"!

Suddenly it occurred to me that he must have a unique view of everything in life. For the most part, he sees the bottom of chairs, tables, drawers. He sees the underside of most things in life. His is a world of trouserlegs and pantyhose.

By contrast we may see the crown of his head, the top of his shoulders. We may even miss looking into his eyes unless we stoop to his level or bring him up to ours. Small wonder that little children are continually reaching to see what is on top of things, where they can't see for themselves.

As they grow taller the distortion between their view and ours is not as great.

In fact, the generation gap may really represent only a few degrees in the angle from which young people see things, but their perspective from that angle may be altogether different. Before we criticize or find fault with them, let's try to see the problem from their point of view.

Too often we think young people should still believe the Santa Claus fable. We must now give them the credit they deserve for their intelligence and insight.

A friend of mine and his wife enjoy a beautiful view out of their front window, including a well-manicured lawn trimmed with colorful plots of exotic flowers and shrubs. To further enhance the beauty of their view, their garden is frequented by hummingbirds that daily make unsolicited rounds of the flowers.

One particular area of the garden, however, lacked sufficient color for the perfect balance they sought. To correct this situation at a time too late for planting, they purchased some artificial flowers. To most outward appearances, these flowers looked real. Only careful inspection would have revealed their synthetic origin.

Anxiously my friends watched to see what the reaction of the hummingbirds would be to the artificial flowers. It was not long before the hummingbirds visited the artificial flowers to check out these newcomers in their garden.

One by one the tiny birds made a pass at the artificial flowers, only to dart quickly away. It took only one quick

look to determine that the new flo
gave off no exotic scent and they prou
had been placed there for superficial and
only and, as far as the hummingbirds were
served no other worthwhile purpose.

Our children are certainly smarter than humm.
They perceive when we are not honest with them. They know
when we are insincere. They can tell when we don't really
care.

Honesty is not only the best policy; it is the only policy —
especially where our children are concerned.

Of Elder Marion D. Hanks' widowed mother it was
said that "she gave her children everything that money could
not buy." Among other things it must have included the
teachings of honesty, sincerity and love — even when they
were most unlovable.

Family ties can be strong only when they include the
sometimes "unlovable," temporarily lost sheep.

CHAPTER 6

Rebellion or Free Agency?

"Man doesn't have to be led into temptation, he can usually find his own way." (Brigham Young.)

One of the most often-quoted scriptures in our Church is that found in section 68 verse 25 of the Doctrine and Covenants:

"And again, inasmuch as parents have children in Zion, or in any of her stakes which are organized, that teach them not to understand the doctrine of repentance, faith in Christ the Son of the Living God, and of baptism and the gift of the Holy Ghost by the laying of the hands, when eight years old, the sin be upon the heads of the parents."

And verse 28:

"And they shall also teach their children to pray, and to walk uprightly before the Lord."

But what about those parents who have taught their children both by example and by precept and yet their children have gone astray? What about those parents who have been faithful in all things, those who have tried to stay close to their children, holding family home evening, those parents who have tried to keep all the commandments in the Church; and yet their children have turned their backs on tradition and have succumbed to peer pressure?

Too often these parents berate themselves, asking: "Where have I gone wrong? Where have I failed?" In most cases they have not failed, but they must remember that these children have their free agency. It is left up to them to choose which way they will go and whom they will follow.

Somehow I think the Lord has a special compassion for these parents. He must understand their tender feelings because He has gone through the same trial Himself. No one can possibly know the anguish God must have felt when His brilliant son Lucifer, a son of the morning, decided not to follow tradition but to oppose the divine plan. Think of God's sorrow, not only when Lucifer departed the ranks of the righteous, but when he took one-third of the hosts of heaven with him.

Undoubtedly the Lord grieved when Cain slew Abel and, in following Satan here on earth, became the first murderer.

How Lehi must have sorrowed over the wickedness of his sons Laman and Lemuel!

And we have a touching account of the sorrow that Alma the Older felt for his wicked son, Alma the Younger. How he fasted and prayed for him, and what great joy he must have felt when Alma the Younger repented! Imagine the anguish Mosiah felt over his sons in their wickedness before they repented.

Someone has said that we, in this modern time, live in an age of softness. We have soft ice cream, soft water, even soft-riding tires. It is possible that this softness has also progressed to our ideals and standards, our character traits.

Where it once was noble to stand up for one's standards, it has now become a mark of peer-admiration to rebel, to destroy, to tear down, to oppose, to be negative, to oppose anything that has stood up for a long time, to abandon standards, ideals and traditions of our fathers. It has become an age of anti-establishment as well as anti- many things. Unfortunately it has not yet become popular to be anti-sin.

Many of the rebellious have been very vocal as they insisted upon their rights—their right to choose, to do and be whatever they wanted. But if one is to be given the right to choose, then one must also accept the responsibility to make a choice and to accept the consequences of that choice. Too often we as parents must stand helplessly by while our children make wrong choices and live the kind of life that these wrong choices lead them into.

So what can we do when those we love turn from tradition and follow the rebellious way? Here are a few suggestions:

1. Let's not turn our backs on them. Someone once said that it takes the warmth of the sun to bring out the bloom of the flower. It may take the warmth of love to bring out the true character in a young man or woman's soul.

One anxious father watched helplessly as his son chose for himself a course totally opposite to what he had been taught. It broke his heart to realize the heartache that lay ahead for someone so close and so dear to him and to be unable to do anything to prevent this. Wisely the father kept his peace and waited for the appropriate moment.

When they were alone one day, the father turned to his son in tears and said: "There are two things we can't change in this life. One is the fact that you are my son and the other is the fact that I love you." The father then assured the son that he would always love him even though he disapproved of some of the things he was doing.

Repentance didn't come right away. There was no immediate miracle or instantaneous turn-around. But years later the son repented and returned to righteous living. The son confessed that one of the great reasons for his turn-about was that his parents loved him when he least deserved it.

2. Have patience. I took my car through a car wash the other day and was somewhat distressed with the fact that it didn't come as clean as it should have. But the attendant remarked that the car was awfully dirty to begin with and that dirty automobiles occasionally had to be sent through the car wash several times before they cleaned up satisfactorily. We recycled our car three times through the car wash before it was adequately cleansed of its dirt and grime.

It may require several recyclings for our children to rid themselves completely of certain habits and return to the life we would like to see them live. This requires patience on their part—but even more so on ours.

The other day I caught a fish that already had another hook in its mouth. In other words, it had been caught once before.

My first reaction was, "What a stupid fish! I can understand its being caught once, but it should have learned its lesson. It should have known better than to be caught a second time."

But as I pondered the problem I realized how premature I may have been in my judgment of that fish. In the first place it had no one to remove the hook. Think how painful it must have been to carry that barbed hook around in its mouth all that time.

Possibly the fish's mouth had been so sore because of the hook that it was unable to eat for a considerable length of time. Possibly the fish was so terribly hungry at the time of the second hook that it just didn't care any more — it might die of hunger anyway.

Furthermore, the fish had no one to teach it that it should avoid such lures, or at least be cautious about them. Its parents may have died in the same way, from a hidden barbed hook in their breakfast.

Think how frightened that fish must have been when it was caught the first time, not knowing that the worm it hungrily swallowed contained a concealed barbed hook. How the poor fish must have struggled almost unto death to free itself from the sharp hook while it was being reeled in by the fisherman.

Lastly, think how relieved that fish must have been when its heroic struggle finally broke the line that first time; when it was suddenly snatched from the jaws of death, so to speak.

This probably sounds like an exaggerated fish-tale, but it also points up the fact that we should be slow to judge each other unless we know the whole story and unless we understand the feelings of the other person. Only when we can place ourselves in their position, knowing exactly what prompted them to do what they did, can we begin to make a judgment about someone's wrongdoing.

"... And forgiving one another, if any man have a quarrel against any: even as Christ forgave you, so also do ye." (Colossians 3:13.)

Be especially tolerant of parents of the rebellious. They need our compassion and prayers, not our criticism or condemnation. Some parents have suffered to the extent of having more than one of their children go astray.

3. Be willing to talk about their problems without becoming angry. Children come to us for hope, not castigation.

The other day we were fishing when the propeller of our boat struck a rock. The boat would move, but only very slowly, and it also became difficult to steer. Before we could tell for sure what was wrong with it, we had to bring the motor out of the water where we could see it.

Fortunately it was an outboard motor and by merely removing a pin we could swing the entire motor upward over the back of the boat so that the propeller and rudder came into plain view. From this angle it was an easy matter to diagnose the trouble. The propeller was broken and the rudder was bent. We were delayed for a time while we straightened the rudder and replaced the propeller. But after the delay we were again on our way and able to travel at the usual speed.

How difficult this situation might have been if we had been unable to see what was wrong or make the necessary repairs!

Young people also need and often *want* the opportunity to bring their misconduct into sight, to take a look at it, to discuss it and to decide what to do about it. They are usually willing to repent, change their ways, start over and get on with life.

But they want to do this without parents becoming so angry about the misconduct that they can't discuss it.

4. Give them moral support. Even nongolfers have heard of sand traps. Sand traps are small, depressed areas

filled with sand, usually alongside the greens on a golf course. If you are able to drive the golf ball straight, to place it exactly where you want it, sand traps are no problem.

But sand traps *are* a problem for those who won't or can't play the game straight. If they drive the ball to one side or the other of the green, the ball lands in a sand trap.

When the ball rolls into a sand trap it burrows into the sand, stops abruptly and rolls no further. Not only that, but when the ball lies semi-buried in a sand trap, the golfer is not allowed to touch it, either with his hand or with his club, to "improve" his lie. He must hit it with his club, blast it out of the trap and onto the green, a feat accomplished only with considerable deftness and skill.

As we mentioned, sand traps are not a problem for those who play the game straight, those who are able to control the ball and avoid devious drives. But it would truly be un-sportsmanlike for others to jeer or deride someone who happens to drive a ball into a trap.

This is the time when everyone needs to "pull for the player" and give him moral support to help him get out of the sand trap.

How much more important is it for us to help those around us who have driven their life into a sand trap! They already know the unfortunate predicament they are in. They may even know what they did wrong that caused their life to land where it is. They undoubtedly feel badly about their entire game of life.

But right now they need our moral support. They need to know that we are "pulling for them"; that we are hoping they will get out of the trap on their first try.

Occasionally we are guilty of negative behavior when our children come to us to confess wrongdoing. They are already aware of the enormity, the seriousness of the offense. They have already been blaming themselves and probably chastising themselves for what they have done.

At this time they do not need a rehearsal by us of their offense. Nor do they need any "I told you so" type of condemnation.

What they do need is understanding and a sympathetic ear that listens, usually without comment, one that is filled with love and compassion. This is no condonement of their misadventure, whatever it may have been, but such an attitude will foster future communication and friendship between you and your children. Your child will know where he can find solace and sympathy and charitableness when he badly needs it.

This is a time when our children need encouragement, inspiration and motivation. The child that is truly motivated is often compared to a wind-up toy. You wind it up, point it in the right direction, then get out of the way and let it run.

If family ties are strong, he will know where he can find the understanding and motivation he needs.

5. Realize how painful the effects of the wrongdoing are to *them*. I recall once when I smashed my thumb rather severely. How that thumb throbbed? There is simply no adequate description of the pain from a smashed thumb! As the blood accumulated under the nail, the pain became even more severe. Even when the acute throbbing ceased, the ache continued. For weeks it was sore and discolored.

Impatiently I watched as the discoloration changed like the shades of autumn from a black to a green to a yellow and slowly back to normal. Perhaps one of the reasons (nonmedical) that a smashed thumb takes so long to heal is to give us adequate time to remember how painful it was and to be more careful the next time we use a hammer.

Our children occasionally "smash their thumb," so to speak, as they grow careless in their conduct. Their conscience often takes a long time to heal, just as with that discolored thumb. Uncomfortable feelings usually remind them of their wrongdoing. But for us to continually rehearse their wrongdoing before them is almost comparable to smashing the thumb again. It is unnecessary, unkind, even traumatic to the young person.

We must realize that some things that seem unimportant to us may be terribly important and vital to them. If you have ever had the experience of hearing your stomach rumble, it sounds considerably louder to you than it does to anyone else. Its importance and its loudness may depend upon how near to the experience a person is. Let's give our children credit for having awareness of the problem and perhaps feeling the impact of the incident more intensely than we do, because of their closeness to it.

6. Be willing to allow your children to make mistakes. If we have already counselled them, we should let it go at that. Let's not try to bend their will. In so doing we sometimes drive them further from us. It is often necessary to let them make mistakes, even though these are costly and painful to them. To us it is obvious that they are mistakes. In their immaturity they don't recognize the folly. But sometimes this is the only way for them to learn.

In one community a huge amount of money was spent to install an incinerator to take care of the garbage and trash. It was felt there would be sufficient salvageable material in the garbage to pay the cost of the incineration of the remaining garbage.

Some doubted the wisdom of this move, since they were certain there would be insufficient salvageable material. And they were right—for a time. It appeared that there was too much garbage to be disposed of to make the venture profitable. But after considerable changing of the mechanics of the incinerator, it finally became a profitable venture. The profit on the operation was so considerable that it more than paid for removal and disposal of the garbage.

Sometimes we have to sit by while our children fill their minds with undesirable material from magazines, movies, television, and other sources. It would appear at times that their minds will become so cluttered with "garbage" that they will have no room left for that which is salvageable, that which is elevating, that which is exalting, and that which would be desirable in the eyes of our Father in heaven.

But if family ties are strong, if rapport is maintained, our children seem to find their way through the maze of mire and mud. Ultimately they verify values and retain that which is good.

7. Remember that even the most difficult child has hidden beauty.

I am reminded of a piece of wood I was given many years ago in a woodshop class in school. We were given a pattern to follow and were told to cut out the piece of wood to fit that pattern. Finally we were to sand and polish the wood to the best of our ability, following which we were to varnish it.

The particular piece of wood given to me contained some knots, which caused unending trouble and effort as I attempted to saw it in the exact form of the pattern. However, when this initial sawing was once achieved, I noticed something special about this particular piece of knotty wood. As I sanded and smoothed the grain of the wood, the pattern of the knots began to stand out. Polishing added to its beauty. Finally, after I had varnished the wood, it appeared more attractive than any other piece of wood in the class—and the knots were the deciding factor. That characteristic which provides most difficulty to overcome is the very thing that makes it most dear and perhaps most beautiful to us.

Sometimes the difficult child develops a more beautiful character because of the "knots" (problems) he or she has had to overcome.

Children with alleged character defects, those who defy tradition, those who stray away from our standards, may cause terrible anguish to our souls. But if we eventually are able to salvage these souls, they may turn out to be more beautiful in character and more precious to us than any of the others— if we have the patience to work with them.

8. Encourage compliance.

Here in the United States we occasionally see road signs which read: "Look out for soft shoulders". This means, stay away from the edges of the road which contain sand or other soft material into which the tires of our car could sink.

In the Bahamas the same warning reads: "Stay away from the verge"; in other words, stay away from the edge of the pavement or we may drop into an abyss.

This applies not only to highways, but also to the road of life. If we venture too close to the verge, if we tempt fate, we may find ourselves sinking in sand and unable to recover ourselves.

We certainly can't force our children to play the middle of the fairway. But we may be able to inspire our young people to stay away from the "verge". We may be able to encourage them not to flirt with fate or dabble in danger.

9. Inspire by the Spirit that God has given you. I watched the other day as my granddaughter played with a magnet and some paper clips. She was playing a game to see how many paper clips she could string from the magnet in a chain-like fashion.

The paper clips themselves contained no magnetism. They were magnetized only as they transmitted the power in chain-like fashion from the first paper clip, the one that touched the magnet.

Sometimes our children are too small to have much power of their own, particularly the power of resistance. But if we have sufficient power ourselves, sometimes we can convey or conduct that same power through our children and even into their children so that they may be able to resist temptation and hang on to that which is right.

I also watched something interesting the other day which involved this same magnet. As my wife was repairing her sewing machine, some small screws fell into our shag carpet. Those screws were so tiny that I was sure they were lost forever. Even if they were able to be recovered in a vacuum cleaner they could scarcely have been found and extracted from the dust of the cleaner itself.

However, my wife quickly brought out the large magnet and drew it several times across the nap of the shag rug. Within an instant the tiny screws literally flew out of the deep nap of the carpet and clung to the magnet.

Such is the power of parents, granted sometimes as they recover children who have forsaken tradition for rebellion. Their affair with rebellion is often a temporary romance, one that they happily give up as they are inspired by the intense power of sincere love of their parents and return to the Lord's ways.

10. Aspire. There is one job to which every parent can justifiably aspire and that is to become a worthy leader of a family. The first step in any program to help the rebellious find his way back is to be a "worthy" parent. There will never be an overabundance of good examples for children to follow. Try to be the type of parent your children deserve.

We are entitled to divine direction as fathers and as heads of our families, if we are worthy.

I recall an experience a friend of mine had:

My friend was already fifteen miles out of town before he was aware of what had happened. As he drove along in his car he suddenly noticed an emptiness in his back pocket, an emptiness that signified the loss of his wallet.

Quickly he pulled to a stop to reflect upon his predicament. Speedily he retraced in his mind his itinerary to determine where he might have left the billfold. Actually it was not so much the relatively small amount of money in the wallet that concerned him. It was his credit cards, his driver's license, his social security card, and his other credentials.

As he drove back to town, his last credit card purchase came into his mind and he headed toward that particular store. At the same time several questions also posed themselves as problems.

If the wallet had been stolen, how many troublesome steps it would require to obtain credentials again! How important his credit rating was! How long it had taken him to acquire the unblemished reputation he had! How important it really was to be trusted, to be accepted anywhere as a good risk, as a customer who would meet his obligations and pay his bills!

My friend then reflected on the importance of possessing a spiritual credit card. Could he qualify for such a card, a card that would entitle him to go anywhere on earth and be accepted as a worthy follower of Christ? Could he obtain adequate references attesting his spiritual worthiness? Could he find people to vouch for his worthiness as a disciple of Christ? Would they attest to the fact that he was not "ashamed of the gospel of Jesus Christ?"

How long might it take to establish such credentials, credentials that would be valid wherever he went on this earth? He also realized that unworthiness could result in a cancellation of this privilege at any time. It would immediately render his card null and void.

Would the spiritual credit card also attest to his worthiness as a husband, as a father, as head of his family?

Fortunately my friend recovered his wallet with everything intact, but not without a new appreciation of it as well as a new determination to remain worthy at all times of his spiritual credit card.

As parents we have the responsibility to do our best to teach, train and inspire our children. But having discharged this responsibility, we should remember that children have their free agency.

They are free to choose which way they will go. Strong family ties help them to make the right choice.

But children might keep in mind that, although they can't choose *their* parents, they can choose the parents of their children — and they can choose, if they wish, strong family ties for *their* children.

CHAPTER 7

Chivalry, Not Chauvinism

I recall when Elder Thomas E. McKay, who had been my mission president many years ago, paid me a visit. It was in the latter years of his life when his health was failing. From my office window I was able to observe him and Sister McKay as their car pulled up in front.

Sister McKay was driving because President McKay's health would not allow him to do so. As the car came to a stop, I noticed that Sister McKay remained seated in the driver's seat. I also noticed that she waited patiently while President McKay, in his infirmity, slowly extricated himself from the passenger's seat.

With the help of a cane in his right hand, and holding firmly to the car with his left, he shuffled around the car to the driver's side. There he opened the car door so that Sister McKay could get out. She then had to assist him, stabilizing his every step as they slowly ascended several steps to my office.

After our amicable visit I observed through the window, as they descended the steps, Sister McKay holding firmly onto President McKay's reluctant elbow to steady him. I could perceive that she slightly nudged him to escort him around to the passenger side, hopefully to help him into the car first. But he would have no part of it!

They made their way slowly around to the driver's side, where he opened the door in his typical, chivalrous-but-now-faltering fashion, allowing Sister McKay to slide into her seat.

After closing the car door he cautiously made his way, with the halting help of his cane in one hand and the steadying support of the other hand on the car, to the passenger's side. There he opened his door and, with considerable effort, climbed in.

Chivalry was ever a part of this man's life — and especially toward his lovely wife. Age and infirmity were allowed no excuse where love and respect for her were concerned. His actions at this time simply bespoke a lifetime of attitudes toward women in general, and particularly toward the woman who was his wife and the mother of his children.

Another busy and successful man I know, a man who could have bought almost any worldly present for his mother, gave her a very unusual birthday present. He realized that her temporal wants were few and that her temporal needs were even fewer. She was comfortable in her home. She was warm. He saw to it that she never lacked for food, clothing or comforts.

But this very perceptive son decided to give his mother the most valuable thing he possessed. In her case this was the very thing she desired most — some of his valuable time.

His birthday card to her, delivered in person, of course, committed him in writing to give her a greater share of his time each week. And nothing could have delighted her more.

A woman I know, a busy housewife, mother, social worker and church worker, was faced with a different problem. Her mother was not only aged, but her one-time keen senses had become dimmed with the years. She could no longer see as well, hear as well, talk as well, or even think as well as she did a few years ago. In fact, her physical condition required that she be cared for in a nursing home.

This compassionate young woman faced a situation that almost precluded verbal communication with her mother and rendered visiting at times extremely difficult. In spite of these obstacles, she resolved to spend more time sitting and holding her beloved mother's hand. At least, her mother would feel the presence and love of her daughter. She might somehow have the assurance that her daughter cared.

With dedication, devotion and tenderness this noble woman carried out her pledge: To give to her mother *of herself.*

Her mother died some months later, knowing and feeling that she was truly loved and appreciated by her daughter. These loving gestures bespeak a love that comes only from close family ties. They transcend all earthly temporal values.

Another man, an executive over hundreds of employees, displayed a different type of nobility. This man could have bought almost anything for his parents. He could have hired several employees to wait on them.

His parents neither wanted nor would have accepted such treatment. But each Sunday morning while others were at church, this important executive slipped into his parents' home and shined their shoes! Nor did anyone discover this act of kindness until after the parents had died.

Still another man, not gifted with beautiful words, in fact a man who finds it difficult to express himself at all, sat down and wrote his wife a lengthy love letter. Grammatically it may have been incorrect. Some of his spelling may have been atrocious. His choice of words surely was not that of an artist, but they were sincere and from the depths of his heart.

In this letter he poured out his love and appreciation to his companion of many years. With humble gratitude he recounted some of her attentive kindnesses, perhaps not even remembered by her, but kindnesses that he could never forget.

We are never too old to be kind, and especially with our spouse. We are never too old to be appreciative. How many people go to their graves with a long list entitled: "Letters I Should Have Written, But Did Not."

We are never too old to be chivalrous. Here is a helpful checklist for husbands:

1. Do you still open the car door for your wife?
2. Do you still assist with her chair when she sits down?
3. Do you help her on with her coat?
4. Do you open the door for her and allow her to go first?
5. Do you take her arm as you cross the street or go up or down a curb, or when you go up or down steps?

And here is a checklist for women!

1. Do you *allow* your husband to open the car door for you?
2. Do you allow him to assist you with your chair?
3. Do you allow him to open other doors for you?
4. Do you allow him and encourage him to take your arm as you walk down the street, or as you cross the street, or as you go up or down steps?
5. Do you thank him when he does these things?

Checklist for both husband and wife: Do you say "Please," or "If you please," or "Thank you very much," or "Excuse me," or "I'm sorry"?

Marriage doesn't become routine or boring on its own. We "routine" it to death when we forget these delightful little courtesies that are like spice to a sauce or perfume to a pretty face.

Chivalry is not limited by time, place, or age. And it does strengthen family ties.

CHAPTER 8

The Importance of Feeling Important

Jane was just thirty-two. Ted was thirty-four. They had three lovely children. Both of these young parents I knew very well, having been in attendance as their three children were delivered.

"But I'm not sure I still love him," Jane said. "It seems as though we quarrel a lot and we just don't have that much in common any more."

After listening for a considerable length of time, I perceived that there was something else Jane wanted to tell me. "Yes, before you ask — there is *someone* else, Doctor," Jane said. "And he is so kind. He thinks I'm important. He notices what I wear. He compliments me all the time. He makes me feel that I am somebody."

Before asking Jane the obvious question, whether her husband ever complimented her, I asked her what her husband did for a living.

"He's an auto mechanic," Jane said. "In fact, he's the best auto mechanic in the city. He can fix anything on any car!"

"Have you ever told him this, Jane?"

"Oh, I think he knows that, Doctor."

"But have *you* ever told him that?"

"No, I don't suppose I have."

"Don't you suppose he might want to hear it from you — that *you* think he's the best in the city?

"I hadn't really thought of that."

"Do you think, Jane, that this might be one of the reasons why he doesn't compliment you as much as you would like to be complimented — because you don't build him up either?

"As for having things in common, Jane, I can think of three things in common that are very important to both of you, some things that you could never have with anyone else. No other man could have given you these three lovely children."

Jane left the office determined to accept the challenge of complimenting Ted every opportunity she could, of building him up, of making him feel worthwhile. She resolved to do this without any thought, at the present anyway, of reciprocation.

"Somehow, Jane, I can't help but feel that compliments are much like bread cast upon the water that certainly will return after many days — perhaps manyfold." (See Ecclesiastes 11:1.)

About a month later Jane returned to the office to report, "Doctor, it does work! I began complimenting Ted and building him up. And it's true that he has begun to pay attention to me. He notices what I wear and he thinks I'm beautiful. I believe we must have started our own 'compliment club'."

Everyone has the need to feel important, to feel wanted, to feel loved. I have often felt that at least part of the marriage ceremony should read: "I hereby accept the challenge to make my spouse feel not only loved but important."

Sometimes it is just as important for a husband or wife to hear the words, "I am proud of you" as it is to hear the words, "I love you."

Most people have the tendency to rise to that which is expected of them. Generally speaking, when complimented for doing well, most people will strive to do their best at all times.

One wife who noticed that her husband's shoes were seldom shined, waited until the occasion arose when he *had* shined his shoes. She complimented him generously and told him how pleased she was at the appearance of his shoes. She noted how much "neater" it made him look, and how much more handsome. Naturally he began to shine his shoes more frequently — in fact, almost every day.

By contrast, a certain woman spent very little time on her hair. She allowed it to become stringy, oily, and in general uncared for. But her wise husband waited until a special occasion for which she did have her hair well coiffed. In fact, as a thoughtful gift for Mother's Day he gave her a coupon to have her hair done at the beauty shop.

After her coiffure he complimented her generously and sincerely about the attractiveness of her hair. Her children also took up the cause and commented that her lovely coiffure surely added to her natural beauty. Naturally she began to take more pride in the appearance of her hair.

Compliment your wife upon the well-dusted areas in the house and the dusty places will become fewer and fewer.

Every husband, no matter how successful he is, has a deep, often unexpressed need to be well thought of — by his wife. She must be his number one fan. He must be important in *her* eyes.

One rather eloquent speaker remarked in confidence that he would treasure one complimentary word from his wife more than all the many accolades he had received from his listeners.

And love will not wear thin unless faults become thick. Someone has said that marriage is where the solo ends and the duet begins. But there are still some stanzas that call for solo parts. It is at these times that the silent spouse can be supportive and interested. "Faultfinding and jealousy narrow the soul, while compliments help both spouses to grow."

One excellent way to dwarf trees is to wrap copper wire around their roots and stunt their growth. Faultfinding can become an endless wire that winds itself around the roots of the soul. It stifles growth and dampens development.

By contrast, compliments nourish the soul, build us up, and make us feel worthwhile. They make us feel important — and everyone needs to feel important.

In our family we have two cars, an older one and a newer model. Both cars have seat belts, but there is an important difference between them. In the newer car there is a buzzer that grinds out an annoying, grating sound that continues to harass until one buckles up. It literally *forces* us to buckle our seat belts. The older car makes no sound and leaves it up to our judgment and memory whether we buckle up or not.

But after driving the newer car for a time and having been forced to buckle up, we have found that we now do this automatically, before we even turn on the key. Something else has happened to us in the process. As a family we discovered that we now buckle up in the older car too, out of habit, without a buzzer to remind us.

It is possible to form the habit of building each other up. We can train ourselves to notice the little things that are so important in making each other feel important. We can learn to be cognizant of kindnesses and to thank each other for thoughtfulness.

As we regularly put forth the effort to compliment and express appreciation for each other, it gradually becomes a habit with us. It becomes a part of our nature to notice the good in everyone and to make them feel important.

A dirt road leading to a tiny town carries this sign at its beginning: "Choose your ruts carefully. You'll be in them for the next eight miles." Let's choose our habits carefully. We're likely to become entrenched in them. We can develop the habit of bringing out the good in each other and making each other feel important.

We have at our house a quart bottle filled with buttons — buttons of all colors, sizes, and shapes, for all purposes.

Rather fascinating, this bottle of buttons, to look at, to study, and even to shake. We have buttons made of bone, plastic, leather, metal, even mink.

But the buttons themselves are almost worthless. No one. would buy them. Who would pay anything for a lot of odd buttons? Probably most people wouldn't want them cluttering up their house.

However, when someone around our home has an important engagement and loses a button from his shirt, pants, dress or blouse, out comes the bottle of assorted buttons!

Spreading these buttons out on the bed, we can usually find one that serves as a fair substitute for the original.

Then how much is that one odd button worth? When sorely needed, a button may be almost priceless.

People are like buttons. They don't find their true worth until they become attached to something and begin to serve.

Some folks are like buttons in the bottle. They may be pretty to look at and even interesting to play games with, but they go through life without serving any useful purpose, just one of many others "on the loose." But God has a purpose for all of His children. It is up to us to become "attached" to some worthy cause and thereby find our true worth in life.

Most people live worthwhile lives. Most people perform many acts of kindness. But for people who are married, perhaps the best thing they can become attached to that will help them to find their greatest worth is their spouse.

One spouse can help the other to realize his or her true worth, and to feel important, sometimes just by expressing appreciation for that person.

As we lose ourselves in service to each other, we will both begin to feel important. Just don't forget to tell your spouse how important he or she is to you!

In a family with strong family ties everyone is important.

CHAPTER 9

Are You Hard of Listening?

Out of Los Angeles comes an interesting report. It seems that police have set up an elaborate system of television cameras at various trouble spots around the city. Experience has taught them just where to expect crime and just where to place cameras to record it.

By monitoring this half-million-dollar surveillance network, police have been able to keep an eye open for trouble when it first happens. In many cases they have stopped it before it became a major crime, while in others they have prevented people from committing serious crimes.

Only a few years ago such a program would have been thought impossible. The mere mention of such an intricate surveillance system would have cast doubt upon the author's credibility. Yet today the program is a reality.

Likewise there are those who question God's ability to know what is going on with His children. They doubt His interest in them as well as His ability to hear and answer their prayers. Yet with His infinite wisdom and His knowledge of all of the laws of the universe, how simple it would be for His own "network" to monitor, analyze, evaluate, and answer our prayers. Not only can God hear our prayers, but just as truly He will answer our supplications.

Too often, however, we ask for guidance and then become impatient and turn off the circuit before the Lord has a chance to give us an answer. Some people try to place a time limit upon the Lord. After a few rings, they hang up.

Perhaps the Lord is pondering an answer. Possibly He is observing our behavior to see if we merit an answer. He could even be testing our sincerity, our patience, and our tenacity. He may even be waiting to see if we have sufficient faith to *expect* an answer.

Sometimes He may find that we have asked Him merely as a courtesy, or a habit, or as a mere formality, not really intending to follow His advice anyway.

On the other hand, sometimes His answer is a definite no, but we refuse to take no for an answer. Be assured that the Lord is there and He has the means to hear and to answer us. But we must also be sure that our receiving set is in good working order so that we will be able to hear Him when He answers us. In other words we need to develop our own sense of listening.

We should remember our own impatience when our children ask us a question. Frequently we fail to answer them immediately when they ask us for or about something. We may be pondering an answer or may be trying to think of a more prudent answer. But let's be certain we don't keep them waiting so long for an answer that they lose interest.

Occasionally our children ask us a question, but because of their short span of attention they run off to play without waiting to receive our answer. In a similar manner we sometimes dial the correct number all right as we call upon the Lord. But after a few short rings of the telephone we hang up, instead of waiting sufficient time for the Lord to answer our prayers.

One person prayed: "Lord, give me patience. And give it to me right now!"

The art of listening, with patience, also applies to praying.

Science has developed all sorts of sophisticated equipment to amplify sounds, to improve one's ability to hear. Tremendous research is continually being carried out to help those who are hard of hearing.

But no one has felt a need to improve our sense of listening. Yet, this may be a more common and a more serious affliction than deafness.

Many parents have been surprised, after listening to their children (for a change), to discover that the children truly have something worthwhile to say. Many parents have been so busy *telling* their children what to do that they fail to *listen* to them. Some parents are so lacking in confidence in their children that they don't give them the chance to see if they can make it.

A story will illustrate this point:

It was an early autumn that particular year, earlier than had been expected. The leaves had hurried through their costume changes with scarcely time for a bow. Now most of them lay in furrows against fences and barns where the wind had blown them.

Seeking wood to carry the family through the winter months, Lon had taken the horses and wagon deep into the hills, beyond the usual wheel-worn trails.

Working with all his strength, Lon had felled several dead trees and chopped them into wagon-load lengths. After carefully securing a chain around his load, he harnessed the horses and headed for home. In spite of his haste, however, time had slipped by and it appeared certain that darkness would overtake him before he could reach the family cabin.

Darkness he had reckoned with, but not a premature snowstorm. No sooner had he yelled "yup" to his team than fluffy flakes began to fall around him. Pulling a knit scarf from the huge pocket of his mackinaw, he tucked it around his neck, buttoned up his coat, and leaned into the storm.

Within twenty minutes the ground was covered and so were the tracks. The landscape was thoroughly whitewashed of all blemishes. But likewise all familiar landmarks had become completely camouflaged.

The falling snow combined with dusky, darkening skies to drop a thick curtain in front of his beloved mountains.

Suddenly everything became a frightening world without direction.

Where should he guide his horses? Was home to the right, to the left — or where? There were no lights, no trails, no shadows, no signs to follow.

Lon could have panicked. He could have simply wept, or even yelled. He could have whistled or screamed. But no one would have heard him.

Lon did none of these things. He remembered something his dad had told him years before.

"If you're ever lost in these hills, Lon," Dad had said, "just give the horses their heads and they'll take you home."

Reaching under the buckboard, Lon pulled out an old tarpaulin he hadn't unfolded for months. Dad kept it there for just such occasions. Climbing under the seat, Lon curled up in the canvas and confidently pulled the old tarp over his head for protection as he yelled: "Yyyyup," and gave the horses their heads. They found their way home!

Too often we find ourselves fearful of the future for our children. Looking around us we see only clouds of confusion and signs of uncertainty. We see temptation towering over and around our youth, appearing to block their vision at every turn.

Occasionally we see them testing first one path, then another, as they grope to find the way they should go. Their uncertainty at times unnerves us. We reach out trying to force them, at times, into our own direction, as we perceive them going in another.

We shed tears as they make mistakes, sometimes serious mistakes — mistakes that could have been avoided. We wonder, when they seem to need help so badly, why they don't consult the map we gave them earlier in their lives.

Ofttimes we shake our heads in disappointment and disillusionment as they seem to forget the warnings we have offered. How could they possibly forget all we have told them, or all we have done for them!

At times like these we might recall what Lon's dad said: "Give them their heads, and they'll head for home." It may take some time, parents, but all that training has not been wasted. In time, in *their* own due time, they'll remember, and head for home.

If you have not been guilty of prejudging and jumping to premature and incorrect conclusions with your children, you are just not average.

I am reminded of one experience I had recently:

The noise was sharp, loud, and unexpected. With a start I sat up in bed.

"Who," I asked myself, "could possibly be throwing rocks on the roof at this early hour. Besides, if they only wanted to waken us, they would throw tiny pebbles, not boulders."

It was barely daybreak in the quiet of the canyon where our summer cabin is located. The sun sneaked a glance through the pines here and there as it slowly rose over the mountain east of the cabin.

Soon there was another sharp report, then another. So loud were the sounds that I feared the roof might be dented by the huge rocks.

Scrambling into my clothes I scurried outside for a look, half-angered at what I considered to be gross inconsideration as well as a prankster-warped sense of humor. A quick look around — no one. A stumbling stroll through the brush surrounding the cabin. Still no one in sight. Now they were playing cute. They must be hiding.

With some sense of shame I now recall that I had already decided in my mind that this must be some young teenagers who thought they were particularly clever — some mischief-minded young vandals bent on causing discomfort to someone they felt sure it would irritate.

As the sound came again, however, the corner of my eye caught something bouncing off the tin roof. It was the same noise, all right, but where was the boulder? I looked again as it rolled along the ground.

No, it wasn't a boulder. It wasn't even a tiny pebble. Disbelieving, I picked up the small, stony-hard, green pine cone from the ground to examine it. Just as I did so, I heard the scolding of the culprit overhead — a bushy-tailed squirrel, who paused only long enough from his harvesting and hoarding of pine cones to tell me to put back what I had taken.

But I had also taken a lesson from the squirrel. How often we pay too much attention to someone who makes a big noise over nothing (like a green pine cone falling on a tin roof), while others, who are efficiently doing their job in life, are simply too busy to make a sound!

How often we take, as an example, some youngsters whose conduct has been out of line and ascribe this conduct to *all* teenagers, failing to take note of the many young people who are dedicated, determined, and extremely anxious to quickly accomplish something worthwhile in this life.

I recall another experience which took place while I was building the aforementioned cabin.

We watched impatiently as the driver unloaded the man-high load of pre-cut lumber. Meanwhile we pored over the directions for assembling our pre-fab cabin. Instructions were accurate but seemed too long for anyone as eager as we were to "see the roof on."

Most of the Lincoln-log-type timber carried a label on the ends to indicate whether it was for side A, side B, etc. But as we proceeded to erect our cabin we continually stumbled over one particular log that didn't appear to belong anywhere. In fact, there was no color or number painted on either end of this log.

Grumbling over this extra, unlabeled log each time we kicked it in our haste to assemble the other logs, we were even tempted to discard it. Then someone said: "A very reliable lumber company manufactures these buildings. They have made thousands and thousands of them. Surely they wouldn't put something in the packet that doesn't belong."

"With them it is a science," someone else volunteered.

Needless to say, we continued to assemble and build as our pieces slowly fell into place and our structure began to take form. Still the unmarked piece was in our way and no one could figure out where it could possibly fit into the building.

Not until all the walls were erected did it suddenly dawn upon us what the troublesome log really was. Not only did it have a place in the structure, it was the main beam for the roof! Upon this beam would rest all of the other crossbeams that would support the roof and the heavy winter snows.

How often we prejudge the Lord's plan for us before we know the entire program! How quick we are to criticize His lack of planning because we personally don't understand the master plan!

How quick we are to judge our children and those around us without knowing their plans!

Certainly no intelligent sports fan would call a baseball game's final score after only one or two innings, or predict a basketball game after the first quarter.

God in His wisdom does have a plan, often known only to Him. He has asked us to have faith in Him and to realize that the plan He has devised for us is the best possible one. It is the plan that will ultimately bring His children back into His presence. He wants us to listen to His prophets as they tell us about His plans for us.

How often we try to call the score of the ball game before it is over, whether it involves our children or the Lord or both! We need the wisdom to listen to our children. We need the patience to stay until they are through talking — to strengthen family ties!

CHAPTER 10

Excuse or Example

We were comfortably seated aboard the huge airliner, seatbelts securely fastened, magazines in hand, and completely relaxed for a long-anticipated flight and vacation. Life was indeed abundant!

Suddenly the stewardess' voice came on the intercom with these rather startling words: "Is there anyone here intending to fly to Denver, Chicago, or New York? If so, you are on the wrong plane!" Many hands went up! Then, for a more certain check, all tickets were carefully re-vouched and re-certified.

There had been a mix-up. Two separate flights going in opposite directions had been directed through the same gate of the small airport and passengers became confused as to which plane they should board. Before take-off the airline wanted to make absolutely sure each passenger was on the right plane and traveling toward the destination he hoped to reach.

Suddenly the thought passed through my mind: "Wouldn't it be tragic to be on the wrong ship in life? Wouldn't it be distressing to suddenly find, in the middle of life's journey, that one had boarded the wrong plane, ship, or train and had spent a good share of one's earthly existence going in the wrong direction?"

It would be even more tragic to find that, as parents, we had taken our family on the wrong plane through life. And whether we like it or not, we are truly the pilots of the plane, at least up to a certain point in life.

Perhaps you will recall the old "bicycle built for two" of years ago. It has now been modernized and is called a "tandem" bicycle. Its popularity is growing each year as we see more and more of them appearing in every neighborhood.

By definition, a tandem is a vehicle in which one is "placed before the other." I had always thought of a tandem as a bicycle on which one "followed" the other. It is obvious that the person on the rear seat must follow the person in front.

The rider in front controls the steering and also the brakes of the bike, while the one in back must pump just as hard, but has nothing to say about where they go or when they stop.

On the other hand, the individual on front has twice the responsibility, since he also controls the destiny — for the moment at least — of the one behind him.

As fathers or mothers, we frequently are sitting on the front seat of the tandem bicycle, with a young son or daughter seated behind us. For that particular time that they ride with us, they go wherever we go.

They see what we see.

They visit the places we visit.

They hear what we say and may follow our example.

They stop and go as we stop and go.

For that particular golden time, we control their destiny.

Whether we desire this great responsibility or not, we mold much of their future thinking, attitudes, loyalties, desires, aims and opinions.

If we examine carefully many of our present inclinations, we may find that more of these than we care to admit were acquired as children from our parents when we "rode tandem behind them" at an impressionable age.

As parents we *must* be out in front, "steering the way" where impressionable minds should go.

Perhaps you have heard of a very special type of plastic called "memory plastic."

As you know, the word *plastic* comes from the Greek language and means "fit for molding." Originally this word was used only to describe various materials which are easily molded or changed in shape by pressure.

Today, however, a new industry has appeared which includes many chemical substances which may or may not be molded and may look like almost any other material we have. In fact, part of the art of plastics is to simulate or imitate other substances such as wood, silk, or rubber, to mention just a few.

The entire subject of plastics changes almost daily with new inventions and combinations of chemicals, and all are exciting and interesting.

One very interesting plastic, for example, is one whose molecules "remember" the shape of the article which they form. For instance, a hairbrush handle made of such "memory" plastic may be heated and stretched out to form a thin rod. But when it is reheated, its molecules flow back to their original position, and it becomes a hairbrush handle again. This "memory" finds many uses, one of which is to shrink tight-fitting pieces of plastic together when they are heated and then allowed to cool.

Boys and girls have some of the qualities of plastics. There was a time when it was thought that the only way to "mold" young people was with "pressure." However, time, experience and wisdom have demonstrated that a few "chemicals" can be added here and a few there that make the plastic more pliable and easier to work.

Some of these "chemicals" are love, understanding, tolerance, patience, and praise. One of the molds into which they can be poured most easily is one called a "good example."

Most young people also have the property of that memory plastic whose molecules "remember" the shape into which they were originally formed. Early training may be temporarily forgotten, but eventually they "remember" who they are and what they are. Hopefully they remember "whose" they are. Then they change back to what they were originally taught to be.

Early training and influence in the home, church, and school may seem to escape some of our young people completely. We may wonder how, with the example set for them along with such excellent training, they could possibly go so wrong. But most of these young people are made up of "remembering" molecules. Eventually their early ideals and training will "pull them back into line." They will help them to "shape up," as we say.

As children, we were taught the value of labeling our possessions for identification. In a family of twelve, this might seem difficult, but all the more essential.

One particular method of identification comes quickly to mind. Although this method was used to mark the wooden handles of all the family tools, I seem to remember it more vividly because it identified our long, family-length Flexible-Flyer sled. The old, no-family-could-do-without-one poker, heated to red-hot in the coal stove or fireplace, was employed to burn the family name into the underside of the sled.

With our name thus etched, we knew that the sled was forever ours. No one could erase the name. Even paint could not camouflage this family trademark. There was no way that our "brand" on the sled could ever be removed. Not only were we proud of that sled, but in such a large family it found almost constant use during the winter months.

Now that the children are grown and have left the home, I don't know what has become of the family sled. But you can be sure that if it is still in use, everyone who sees it knows unmistakably to whom it originally belonged.

As parents we also place our "brand" upon our children. Hopefully this is done knowingly and thoughtfully. Perhaps it may be done inadvertently without our realizing that we have placed our mark upon them.

It can be done with words. It can be done with deeds (example). It can be done with gestures. Most surely it can be done with attitudes. Even a raised eyebrow can leave its indelible imprint upon a receptive soul.

Let's think back in time to recall certain ways in which our parents may have left their "trademark" upon our lives.

For instance, my father's example of industry, his philosophy of giving more than a day's work for a day's pay, burned itself deeply into the minds of his children.

Unselfishness and compassion for the unfortunate were traced and retraced upon our consciences by his many examples of "neighbor-loving" and neighbor-helping".

Unquestioned faith in God, as observed in the simple supplications to God by our parents as we knelt together in good times and bad, carved a very special, meaningful and lasting, life-directing mark upon our hearts.

The humble assurance derived from fasting and praying together sustained our family through illnesses, operations, disappointments, and even through the death of our loved ones.

Respect for God's servants became a natural and sincere attitude as these men were honored and upheld by our parents in their important calling. As children who observed the regular payment of the tithe in our parents' home, we found it easy to continue this practice in our own homes.

We bear the mark placed on us by our parents' observance of the Sabbath. If the mark does not always provoke us to observe the Sabbath day to keep it holy, it certainly pricks our consciences painfully when we do not.

Yes, loyalty, love, courtesy, consideration and compassion are deftly etched upon tender, youthful minds by years of unspoken-yet-understood devotion between parents as they wittingly or unwittingly shape, fashion, and mold the final proud family "trademark" upon their most precious possessions, their children.

We have all heard parents say, "Guess we didn't teach our children very much." Actually they taught them a great amount, probably much more than they realize. Whether by word or deed, we are constantly teaching our children.

Another experience may illustrate this point:

The day was hot and the trail was dusty. My daughter and I were riding the final half mile of an exciting though exhausting trip into the hills on our trail bikes.

Suddenly something glimmered in the setting sun a few yards ahead of us. Within seconds we reached a three-foot water snake, slithering slowly across the powdery road. As we paused to watch it lazily disappear into the tall grass bordering the road, our eyes caught sight of the faint trail the snake's body had sculptured in the dust behind it.

There was no mistaking this trail for any other. It was shallow, it was narrow, but most striking of all, it was crooked. A snake's winding path in the dust is unlike any other.

As if by prearranged contrast, at this same moment a 707 jet zoomed overhead, tracing its arrow-straight stream of vapor behind it. Here was yet another unmistakable trail.

But how like ourselves is this simple pattern. Behind every man lies the path he has taken, marked here and there with tell-tale signs of his passing. In most cases his path is stamped along the way with his special trademark. These signs are characteristic of him and his peculiar ways. Unmistakably they are his. Nor can they be attributed to any other.

How true it is that we may die, but our works, be they good or bad, live after us.

Benedict Arnold's trail has become the hallmark of the traitor. Judas Iscariot is not remembered as a disciple of Christ. The trail he left marks him forever as a betrayer.

How different history might read if Pontius Pilate had mustered the courage of his inner convictions! Instead of being known as the one who, cowed by pressure, released Christ to an aroused, misinformed, and angry mob, he might forever have been acclaimed as the Savior's noble and fearless defender.

King Agrippa, wicked though he was, could have turned the tide of opinion among his subjects in favor of the Christians if he had not been a weak-willed "almoster" as he said to Paul: "Almost thou persuadest me to be a Christian."

Then consider the trails left by Peter, Paul, Stephen the martyr, Martin Luther, and many other men of courage who stood up (or even gave their lives) for what they believed. Their trail, like the path to the moon, has been set and will be followed by other courageous men to come.

What trail will you leave behind when you depart from this life? For what will you be best known?

Yes, we continually and mostly by example leave a trail. But whether it is the crooked trail of a snake or an arrow-straight trail of a jet is up to us. And we may be certain that this trail is likely to influence the future path of our children.

The responsibility of building a conscience in our children is also ours. They usually form their standards and their habits based upon that which they have learned from us, either by word or example, usually when they are very young.

One experience taught me very well how much more powerful example can be than words.

"What is that double line in the middle of the road for, Dad?" asked one of my young sons, as we traveled the highway on one of our frequent trips together.

"That means: 'Don't pass another car'," I answered. "When you see the double lines, there is usually a curve, or a hill, or a blind place in the road. If a car swerves out around another car to pass it in such places," I continued, "it could easily have a head-on collision with a car coming in the opposite direction. It's there for your protection. Never cross a double line to pass a car!"

The boy was satisfied with the explanation and I was secretly pleased that I had taught him another lesson in safety.

Several minutes later my son remarked: "Dad, you just crossed a double yellow line."

I *had* crossed a double line! I was embarrassed.

Through my mind sped a host of self-effacing, self-justifying explanations about why I had crossed the double line—but they sounded like pretty weak excuses.

Then I realized that if I began to justify myself in breaking the law, my son would do the same thing if he broke the law. It was a tight and tense situation!

My son had the goods on me and there was no way out. There was nothing to do but confess my guilt and negligence — and promise to be more careful in the future.

It sounds so good when we tell our children about laws and the importance of obeying them. But children are just like adults — they would "rather see a sermon than to hear one any day."

The next time we go thirty-five miles per hour in a twenty-five-mile zone, or the next time we slide through the stop sign without making a complete stop, we are teaching our son or daughter the wrong way more effectively than if we gave them a dozen lectures.

Let's ask ourselves an honest question as often as we honestly should: "Are we setting a good example?" "Are we crossing a double line?"

Another experience comes clearly to mind:

It was the last mile or so before turning onto the freeway. There were few cars on the highway. It was a downhill grade. Unconsciously I peered over the steering wheel at the speedometer and quickly slowed my car to the proper speed. Unwittingly I had allowed it to exceed the limit as it gained speed down the long hill.

With a pang of conscience I hurriedly looked in the rearview and side-view mirrors but could see no one. I was relieved that the road seemed devoid not only of other cars but especially of police cars, in view of my having exceeded the speed limit.

Proceeding down the highway about a mile I came upon a car parked on the side of the highway. Suddenly a man in uniform stepped out into the center of the road and waved a red flag, a sign for me to stop.

Very courteously the officer asked to see my driver's license. At first I surmised it might be a simple traffic check for drivers' licenses, a not too uncommon procedure. But when the officer began to write in his ticketbook, my natural question was: "What did I do wrong?"

Without another car on the road I felt certain that my earlier speed had not been clocked, even by radar.

"You were doing seventy-four in a sixty-five-mile zone, sir," he said, as he read my mind.

Since I was certain of my lawful speed during the last mile or so, I wondered how they could possibly have known of the excessive speed prior to that last mile. The question still posed itself in my mind, "How did they know!"

"You were clocked by radar in our airplane overhead, sir," the officer said before I had a chance to ask.

Well, the citation proved to be only a warning, but it was justifiable and served well its purpose to slow me down and cause me to watch my speed more carefully in the future. It would help me to stay within the law.

As I drove away following the courteous warning by the highway patrol, the thought crossed my mind how very like life this experience had been. Too often we look around us to see if anyone is looking, or at least if there is anyone we know, anyone in whose presence we might be embarrassed. Then we proceed to act accordingly.

Usually, however, we forget to look up. In so doing we forget that the Lord cares how we act, how we conduct ourselves, whether we obey the heavenly laws or not. We are really never alone, nor are we ever in a situation in which our conduct is not important, least of all in the presence of our children.

The next time we look around us to see if anyone is there, let's not neglect to look up!

If we start our children out right with correct principles, they will find it easier and better to build upon these principles.

I recall some years ago an experience I had:

It was really only a shed I was building, but for me it represented my first real attempt at construction — on my own. I had watched carpenters work and decided this was something I must learn. And it looked so easy the way they did it.

The first few boards went together without a hitch. Carefully I had measured them with my tape. As meticulously as possible I sawed along the line. Each nail was well placed and hammered so that no marks defaced the wood.

But then something went wrong. A board must have slipped. Suddenly nothing seemed to fit into place. When one joint didn't fit I tried to compensate at the next one and discovered that none of them fit from then on.

Finally I sought the advice and help of a seasoned carpenter. One look at the structure told him of my folly.

"Regardless of what you build, there are several things to keep in mind. First, be sure you have a solid foundation upon which to rest the structure. Next, you need two important tools in addition to your hammer and saw. These are a spirit level and a square. If any of your joints are not square and your structure is not level to begin with, you are headed for trouble. Nothing will fit from that point on."

The carpenter shook his head as he viewed the ill-planned shed.

"Let's take it apart and start over again. But this time we'll begin with a solid foundation and see to it that every board is true to the spirit level and every joint on the square."

It seemed so easy when a master craftsman did it. But I noticed how carefully he checked each step of the way with his spirit level and his square.

I couldn't help but think how very much like this our lives are. One compromise calls for another, and yet another, until we have no principle left, and no similarity to that noble character we started early in life to become. On the other hand, if we give children a good solid foundation of righteous, uncompromising principles upon which to build, they have the beginning of a well-planned and probably a successful life.

If they are taught to square with everyone they meet, and if their spirit is on the level, they can build their lives brick by brick, knowing that these bricks will fit together solidly.

Not only will their lives be easier and more satisfying but life will be a masterpiece of which they can truly be proud.

If we can inspire our children enough to keep them on the right track, there is a good chance they will pursue that same course after they are grown.

May I share another experience from which our family learned:

It was a pretty wild ride. There were times when the car seemed to leave the track and fairly sail through the air. The wheels became momentarily silent as we glided breathlessly, suspended in space, only to land once more on the track. Suddenly we were pulled to the right, then around another curve to the left as we raced over the thrill-packed route of the "Mine Tunnel Ride," at the huge resort.

Our stomachs flattened our backbones as we dipped, ascended, speeded and slowed. Finally the ride was over. Looking backward over the greased track it did not seem possible that we could have traversed the course in such a few seconds!

Unable to resist the temptation, I had to see what held us on the path. What ingenious device was there to keep us from pitching headlong through the air?

Closely inspecting one of the pipe-shaped circular tracks, I first noticed an unmistakable tracing on its underside. Turning the inspection to the "mine-tunnel car" itself, I discovered the safety secret of the wild ride at "Six Flags Over Texas." Sturdily and securely welded into the undercarriage of each car was a "safety wheel." This wheel traversed the underside of the circular pipe rail at such an angle that it was literally impossible for the car to leave the track without first removing this wheel.

Every ordinary wheel was counterbalanced with a safety wheel that kept it on the track. So long as this wheel was in place and functioning, the car could not get off the track.

Each of us has a safety wheel in life that, if kept in place and functioning, will keep us from getting off the track spiritually. This wheel even has a name. It is called the safety wheel of Church activity. As long as we keep this wheel well oiled and securely welded into its proper place in our lives so that we can use it, it will keep us from becoming too worldly, from getting off our spiritual track.

It will keep us from becoming "spiritual dropouts," from leaving the path that God has laid out for us in this life. It will "steer" us home to dwell eternally with our Father in heaven.

But our children will look to us to set the example for them to follow. To send our children to church while staying home ourselves is hypocritical, to say the least. It is tantamount to saying: "It is good enough for you but not good enough for me." Let's take instead of send our children to church. Let's set the example for them.

Another responsibility that we as Latter-day Saints assume when we have children, is to convey or bequeath to them a testimony of the divinity of Jesus Christ. A parent who has not confronted his son or daughter, eyeball-to-eyeball in a serious moment and borne solemn witness of the divinity of Jesus Christ, has in very deed missed a glorious opportunity and an unmatched experience.

My neighbor has a tiny gas light in a new lamp post in front of his house. In the daytime it appears to go out, but that is merely because the sunshine, by comparison, is so bright. It is such a tiny flame that one wonders how it could possibly give off sufficient light to be of any value whatsoever to anyone at any time.

Yet in the middle of the night when all about us is so very dark, this tiny flame shines up and down the street, emitting its welcome light throughout the entire neighborhood. Faithfully it lights the way for those who come home late, and for those who arise before daylight to go to work. It is a friendly little oasis in a great desert of darkness. It pierces the night and challenges the blackness like the open doorway to a warm and hospitable home on a dark and forbidding wintry night.

Our children will sooner or later be confronted with darkness all about them. They may stand alone in their beliefs, in their principles, in their standards. They may be subjected to considerable criticism, and even abuse, because of their beliefs.

But the tiny light of testimony which has been implanted in their hearts when they were young (usually by their parents) can uphold them in these periods of darkness. Not only will this testimony prove to be a haven of hope to sustain them, but it will point the way home when they seem to be lost. This friendly little light burning within them tells them that hope is not gone, that there is a God in the heavens who hears and answers their prayers. And it tells them they have a Savior who cares what happens to them.

Let those of us who are blessed with a testimony of Jesus Christ not hide this light under a bushel, particularly as far as our children are concerned. One of the greatest factors in the development of a testimony of Jesus Christ in young people is whether or not their parents have one — and whether the children have heard them express it.

Let me cite another analogy to illustrate the value of a firm testimony in parents:

I can still remember the day!

We stood back and admired that for which we had waited so long. The rich blue and green colors contrasted with the white walls and almost reminded me of how green fields must look in the springtime . . . in heaven. Gone was the lusterless linoleum, the floors that had to be periodically scrubbed. At long last, we had wall-to-wall carpeting!

Never would we tire of walking barefoot through the house just to remind ourselves of its soft elegance. Willingly would we vacuum where we had laboriously mopped and polished. In the kitchen, the halls, yes, even in the utility room where washer and dryer stood like majestic marble monuments, we had wall-to-wall carpeting.

To make this carpeting even more luxurious we had specified a double-thick padding. That ankle-deep feeling as our feet traversed this new badge of affluence was the culmination of years of longing. We wanted to enjoy it to the fullest.

Our worries were over. Or so we thought. But something unexpected appeared in the utility room as the first batch of washing was turned on and went into its spin. Suddenly the always dependable washer began to waltz, then swing, and finally convulse as it bounced around on its unsteady base of heavy rubber padding.

This should be no problem. A little adjustment was all it would need. But still it writhed as it washed. A sheet of plywood over the carpet and underneath the washer, unwelcome and even repulsive as it might be to us, should do the trick. But still the washer hummed and shimmied as it rocked and rolled all over the floor.

Next, a sheet of heavy plywood was nailed to the floor — over the carpeting and the padding. Still it was unsteady. Screws were placed through this wood and into the floor to firm up the sheets of plywood. But there remained a disquieting amount of play and vibration because of the rubber padding!

Only when the carpet was reluctantly removed from under the washer and the heavy machine once more anchored to a solid footing did it deliver its usual impeccable performance. Only then could its machinery function in the way it was intended.

To avoid becoming "wobbly" like the washer, everyone needs to be anchored to something solid. The most solid, unwavering thing to which a family can be anchored is the gospel of Jesus Christ. If a family is to have strong, unwavering ties, it should anchor itself to the Church. But the chain that tethers us to that anchor is an unwavering testimony. Parents who have a "wobbly," wavering, and insecure testimony cannot hope to give their children anything but a wobbly testimony.

Parents must set the sail and determine the course. Children won't always follow, but the parents will at least know that they have started them in the right direction.

Finally, regardless of how inadequate some of us may feel as teachers, we are still the most influential teachers our children have. We are teaching them almost every minute we spend together. They are learning from everything we say and do — whether it is an excuse or an example.

For those of us who feel that we do not know enough to teach our children, may I remind you of something a very wise person once said: "Children don't really care how much you know until they know how much you care."

Their activity in the Church may be in direct proportion to yours. But of one thing you can be certain: A good example strengthens family ties.

CHAPTER 11

Commonsense Communication Versus Stubborn Silence

It was a tight ball game all the way, with one of those cliff-hanger endings that kept everyone on the edge of his seat. The score was tied and it was the top half of the ninth with two out, nobody on, and Mike was up to bat.

Mike's record spoke for itself. He had come through before and he should be able to do it again. He had been in tight places before. In fact, some thought he could do it with one hand tied behind him, but there were others just as sure he would strike out.

So determined was he to homer it, though, that he missed the ball altogether; and not once, but twice. Two strikes, and only one more chance to do or die.

Carefully, cautiously, even a bit nervously Mike sized up the next pitch. Then, wham! and away it went, heading for the fence. It was over the fielder's head, but he was after it, and quicker than Mike thought possible. In seconds he had the ball on its way to the catcher to nail Mike as he came into home plate.

A quick glance over his shoulder as Mike rounded third convinced him that he probably could and should try to make it home. He would slide in under the catcher and complete that much-needed home run. Down the line he came in a wide arc right over third base and heading for home with all he had, when he saw the ball out of the corner of his eye and knew he had to think of something to get him home safe.

He would start for one side, then quickly maneuver to the opposite side as he out-finessed his opponent. He started for the left, drawing the catcher with him and off balance as he reversed his plunge to the right and slid toward home plate. But he was counted out as the catcher tagged him.

A brilliant hit, a masterful strategy, good thinking, but *he missed home plate* and the game was over.

Regardless of the loss it was a great game and Mike is still one of the outstanding players. *But the game was lost because he didn't touch home plate.*

Would you believe that it's possible for husband and wife to live together year after year and never really touch home plate in their communication? Too many marriages have been lost for this same reason. After many years one spouse may say to the other: "You've never really understood me," or "I can't talk to you," or "You don't listen." They probably did communicate at one time, but they have just forgotten.

But it's also possible that we sometimes talk *around* the subject rather than *to* the subject. As a result we don't really convey what we are thinking or that which we want to tell our children or our spouse. Let's consider an analogy:

Man has learned much about communication from observing animals. Whether crowding each other by body contact at the feeding trough or signalling by means of subtle, unspoken, almost unnoticed gestures, messages are passed sometimes silently, sometimes quite noisily, from animal to animal.

Consider, for example, the communication between male and female moth by an odor that can be detected over a distance of half a mile. Or observe bats or porpoises as they employ intricate animal sonar transmission and reception, both for finding objects and for communicating with each other.

Goats and sheep, by contrast, warn each other by stomping their feet when in danger. And nearly every hunter at some time or other has been completely disarmed by the sudden, unnerving whapping of a pheasant's wings as it noisily lunges into a "take-off" right beneath his feet. By frightening the hunter the pheasant not only hopes to save his own life, but he is also warning other pheasants that danger is near.

A beaver's unanticipated tail-flailing "splat" against the water can chill the blood of nearly any fisherman or trapper. At the same time it warns other beaver, including its own young, to run for hidden cover.

Mother hens cluck constantly to let their carefree chicks know that Mom is nearby. Or consider the baleful "baa" of sheep who have temporarily lost sight of their lambs. On the other hand recall the cry of distress when the young of any brood are frightened or find themselves in danger.

Isn't it strange then that man, who among all animals has developed the most intricate means of communication with others, a communication that enables him to contact other men almost any place upon the earth — or even in space — often has the most difficulty in maintaining communication with his own family?

A scowl, a smile, an eyebrow lowered in scorn or raised in approbation — how often and how greatly our life and our happiness depend upon these! How important it is to maintain this communication with each other!

How many physicians can give explicit instructions to their patients, yet have difficulty telling their wives how much they love them!

How often an attorney can thoroughly analyze a case at law, present a logical defense so crystal clear that the jury can be swayed in his direction by the particular picture he paints for them! Yet this same lawyer has difficulty in telling his wife how he feels about her.

Many top executives control the fate of thousands of employees. Many personnel officers specialize in interviewing and communication. Yet how many of these have difficulty in telling their wives how much they love them!

One young girl was asked what she wanted more than anything else in life. Her answer was not for any of the frivolous things of life. She simply said: "I just wish that I could really talk to my mom!"

I recall once when we visited Boston by auto:

"Just make a left turn, then enter the tunnel," we were told. The directions seemed so simple, and they probably were simple for local Bostonians. But after making the turn, we found there were several tunnels — and unfortunately we took the wrong one. Thus began our "See-Boston-by-Tunnel Tour," an unplanned excursion during which we traversed nearly every tunnel in Boston, not once but several times.

Usually we had no sooner entered a tunnel than we discovered it was the wrong one. But in Boston traffic there was no turning back, and of course no turning around. The traffic moved at "Grand Prix" speed and we moved nervously with it. And we drove at this speed for a long time before we found an exit from which we could escape the tunnel traffic.

I don't know how much it cost us in tolls and time, and this is not really important now. But we did learn a priceless lesson. "Be sure you are heading for the right tunnel before you enter it," we agreed, "for there is no turning around in a tunnel."

"I know I was going in the wrong direction," a morally-misdirected young man told me recently, "but I simply couldn't turn around once I had started." He had begun his journey with the wrong companions who took him in the wrong direction in the wrong tunnel.

"I wanted to stop what I was doing," he said, "for I knew it was against everything I had ever been taught. I felt uncomfortable and unhappy living that kind of life, but I couldn't find a way out. I couldn't find an exit to get off my riotous racetrack."

Now, many heartaches later, he has filled his bag of regrets to overflowing. Remorse has become his relentless companion. Finally he has found his way out of the tunnel, but not without paying a dear price in time, and not without cluttering his mind and soul with a catalogue full of unpleasant memories.

We must realize that sometimes our children, sometimes our spouse, and sometimes ourselves, are caught in a tunnel or a series of tunnels, and we can't turn around, at least not right away.

But there must always be an end to any tunnel. If we are patient, we will be able to exit, to turn around, to change our direction. Richard L. Evans, in profound wisdom, said: "If we don't change our direction, we'll end up where we're going."

Meanwhile it will require our patience, love and understanding with that person who is on the wrong track or going the wrong direction. This so-called "tunnel time" is a time when communication is especially important.

To fully understand communication, however, we need to realize how difficult it is for some people to communicate. They are unable to express their feelings, whether love, anger, or any other feeling.

Have you ever been involved in a mass departure, either of young people going into the service or young men going on missions? If so, observe how some of them are extremely expressive and emotional. Others stand there uncomfortable and uneasy because of their inability to express their feelings.

Sometimes these people come from homes where feelings were never expressed. Feelings may even have been suppressed and regarded as something unhealthy or even disgraceful.

When someone touches a hot stove he is not anxious to get near anything hot again. Cautiously he will avoid anything that even suggests heat. Likewise someone who has had his feelings "burned" by expressing himself or herself and then being rejected, will hesitate to project those feelings again.

It is important that we understand this type of behavior when we discover it in our children, in our spouse, in our friends, or even in ourselves. We must understand that some individuals can only love in silence.

For the rest of us it is important to communicate with each other easily and frequently so that small differences are not allowed to grow into enormous problems that no longer have a solution.

I recall when we moved into our new home in which there was a retaining wall abutting the patio. Where the two joined each other there was a tiny crack in the cement. Since the contractor had guaranteed his work, I was anxious that he not be subjected to undue expense. Therefore, I suggested that he caulk this crack before moisture entered it, froze during the winter, and split the seam wider.

He agreed it should be done, but for some reason did not get around to caulking the crack before winter came. By the following spring the tiny crack had expanded to a separation four to five inches wide, bordered by an unsightly, crooked retaining wall that had to be replaced at considerable, unnecessary cost.

How simple it would have been to mend the crack while it was still tiny!

Likewise in our communication — if we can talk things over early, before unkind things are said, before feelings are hurt, before scars are inflicted that are difficult or impossible to be removed, this is the better way.

According to Dr. Victor Richards' book, *Cancer, the Wayward Cell,* cancer cells have lost their ability to communicate. Whereas normal cells communicate with the cells surrounding them, cancer cells do not. In fact, a galvanic current will not pass through cancer cells because of their refusal to communicate with each other.

Suppose we skin an elbow. Normal cells set about to repair the damage. Each cell grows, divides and provides more normal cells to replace those lost in the injury.

But when the damaged tissue has been replaced, when healing is complete, the cells agree among themselves (by communication) that no more repair is necessary. They then stop the repair work and merely keep up normal maintenance.

By contrast, cancer cells pay no attention to each other. A cancer cell couldn't care less what its neighbor cell is doing or how any repair work is coming along. It is concerned only with itself and its own welfare.

Without any consideration for other cells, or even the body as a whole, each cancer cell continues to grow, divide, and multiply, piling up a huge amount of tumor tissue that eventually causes death of the individual — and incidentally the ultimate death of the cancer cells too.

Communication is necessary for complete cooperation between cells. But it may be even more necessary if individuals are to live together in peace and happiness.

How much more important is it then for husband and wife to communicate with each other? For a successful marriage, and certainly for a successful family, husband and wife must stand elbow to elbow, communicating frequently with each other on nearly every problem that comes along. Without such communication the marriage will not succeed, nor will the individuals be happy. When communication breaks down, love dies of starvation.

There is also something to be said for nonverbal type of communication.

Celia and Jack had three children. The five of them sat next to each other in church. I noticed that, whenever possible, interspersed with caring for their three lovely children, Jack quietly stole Celia's hand, even if it was only to interlock their little fingers. Sometimes a gentle squeeze conveyed his love and admiration for this the mother of his children and the sweetheart of his life.

Several times when the speaker alluded to the love between husband and wife, I again noticed a gentle squeeze that conveyed the feeling, "I love you."

When it became necessary to take Johnny their tiny son to the restroom, a quick nod of the head indicated that Jack would take care of this problem. Throughout this service, and I am certain on other occasions, Jack and Celia carried on an entire conversation without uttering a word — a conversation of love and understanding.

It is not necessary for all feelings to be expressed, however. In spite of the fact that silence sometimes seems awkward, silence may be preferable to the utterance of something that would hurt or offend, even though it may be true.

Some very wise person has said that the difference between a very successful marriage and one that is mediocre consists of four or five things a day left unsaid.

But good communication strengthens family ties!

CHAPTER 12

Placing Prayer in Proper Perspective

It had been an interesting and inspiring interview. My friend had said, "I made my decision to let God steer the course of my life, and this He has done!"

Through God's help he had overcome his alcoholism and he felt that his experience could now be beneficial to others. Giving up his lucrative and responsible job as an industrial consultant, he had moved his family to another state, and with less than 30 percent of the salary he had previously enjoyed he worked for the rehabilitation of alcoholics.

"Naturally there have been some obstacles and some heartaches, but I lost interest in making money long ago. I would never trade the satisfaction I now have in helping people to find themselves again." His success in this field has been no less than astonishing.

Sitting in my parked car following the interview, I marveled at the dedication of my friend. I pondered over the meaningful words I had heard from this remarkable man, "Let God steer my life!"

As I pulled back on the steering wheel to shift my position on the seat, I heard the wheel click into a locked position. Truly the car was not to be steered any place as long as the ignition remained off.

As soon as I turned the ignition key, the steering wheel could be moved — but only with difficulty. When I started the motor, the power steering immediately took over, allowing me to turn the wheels with great ease as I maneuvered the car out of the parking lot.

But it wasn't until I was sailing along the highway that I noticed how effortlessly the car could be steered wherever I wanted it to go. With only the gentle caress of a finger, the steering wheel faithfully moved in whichever direction I desired it to go.

Only then did the true meaning of my friend's words return to me: "I made a decision to let God steer the course of my life." Many of us would like to have divine direction in our lives. We have only good intentions, and surely it would be desirable to have our lives so ordered.

But have you ever tried to steer a parked car with the ignition off and the steering locked in place? Sometimes we turn our lives over to the Lord in this condition. But my friend not only turned his life over to God; he had turned on the ignition, started the motor, and had the car running before he said: "Show me what direction you want me to take."

I asked myself: "Would I be willing to give up my profession, relocate my family, reduce my standard of living, work only with people my profession has generally shrugged off as 'beyond help'? Would I really turn my life over to God to use as he saw fit?"

At this moment of my soul-seaching I am rereading Matthew 19:21: "Jesus said unto him, if thou wilt be perfect, go and sell that thou hast, and give to the poor, and thou shalt have treasure in heaven: and come and follow me."

But the honesty in my soul is still dwelling on the following verse: "But when the young man heard that saying, he went away sorrowful: for he had great possessions."

Wouldn't the Lord be pleased to hear someone say (for a change), "And now Lord, is there anything I can do for you?"

Just as we sometimes ask the Lord to steer us in the proper direction and then fail to take that direction, sometimes we pray halfheartedly, not willing to give of ourselves completely.

Sometimes we pray for direction, receive all the instructions, then refuse to move our feet.

It reminds me of an interesting rug sale my wife and I once attended.

There was something captivating and exciting about that sale. Colors were bright, dull — sometimes even exotic. Patterns varied from drab to psychedelic and thicknesses ranged from mini to maxi. But although there were many colors, patterns, thicknesses, and qualities to choose from, the buyer was definitely limited as to size.

The reason for the limitation on size was that this particular sale was a remnant sale, a sale of "left over" rug pieces. After people have bought the amount they need to carpet a specific room, hallway, stairway, or even their entire house, that which is left becomes a remnant, also known as the "couldn't use" or "seconds." These are the pieces that can't qualify to sell as first grade because of their limitation in size.

At such a sale it is frustrating indeed to find just the right color in just the desired pattern, with thick, quality nap, and then discover that there is not quite enough to cover the area you want it for. The joy of the bargain is soon lost when one realizes that this is only a remnant, a "left over" that is simply too small for his needs. Naturally that is why it is so cheap.

But many of us do this same thing with our lives. Selfishly we first take out of it what we want for ourselves and our own personal whims. Only after we have satisfied our own wants do we finally get around to saying: "All right, Lord, here is my life (what's left of it), and if it doesn't interfere too much with what I already have planned, take it and do with it what you want."

Sometimes we forget that life itself is a gift from God. We also forget that when we turn our lives over to God, He is usually very generous in giving us back much more than we turned over to Him.

If we truly want the Lord to steer our lives and help us to achieve happiness, we must give Him something to work with.

We must not give Him only a remnant that may be too small for the job He has in mind for us.

Perhaps the same thing applies to us when we pray for something but are not willing to make the sacrifice necessary to permit our prayer to be answered.

We ask the Lord to help us to be more charitable with others, to be more kind and considerate with our spouse, or to be more patient and understanding with our children. Then, expecting the Lord to work some magic for us, we forget our own role in making the change and remain critical and unforgiving as we deal with our fellowman.

Sometimes we feel we don't receive the answer to our prayers. But it may be that we fail to listen long enough, intently enough, or accept the answer that our Father in heaven gives us.

On one occasion Pat Boone's daughter was praying. After some pause she said: "Speak a little louder, Lord. I can't hear you."

But whether we receive a direct answer to every prayer or not, it is impossible to kneel down with one's spouse, arm in arm, in the sincere attitude of prayer, supplication and forgiveness, and not stand up a better person.

Sometimes we pray for inspiration and are so surprised to find our request has been granted that we hesitate to follow it.

One intelligent young mother was preparing her lesson for the Spiritual Living class in Relief Society. As she studied the lesson she read and reread it. Prayerfully she prepared herself, but somehow she felt this was not the lesson she should give at this particular time.

Again she prayed for that feeling of satisfaction and serenity that comes when one knows that she is doing what the Lord wants her to do. But again she felt that this was not the lesson she should prepare.

Once more she knelt in prayer and said: "Father, if this is not the lesson I should give, help me to know what I should prepare." As she again began to study for her lesson, the words came into her heart almost faster than she could write them. The new lesson almost outlined itself.

When she presented that lesson, one young mother, a divorcee, came up to her and said: "How is it possible that you would know exactly what was troubling my heart? You have given me the answer to my prayer."

We should remember that God's ways are not man's ways. Sometimes the answer we receive may not seem entirely logical to us. But if it is given by the Lord we should follow it.

The Lord has told us that if any of us lack wisdom, we may ask Him. But He says we must ask in faith. (James 1:5.) This applies as we seek wisdom concerning our families too.

One of the pressure tactics of the Russians in their cold war with democracy was to "snow" the radar in the twenty-mile-wide air corridor leading from West Germany to isolated Berlin.

The Communists knew how vital these airlanes were to the United States and its allies. Also they realized that without them West Berlin could be cut off totally from the West.

We then would have to get out of Berlin, and abandon the thousands of freedom-loving people there who depended on us.

This "snowing" was accomplished by dropping myriads of small metallic strips into the sky along these corridors. The strips produced a barrage of white streaks across the pilot's radar screen.

In this way they intended to make it dangerous or even impossible for western pilots to fly to Berlin. The pilots called these metal strips "chaff" or "garbage." However, experienced pilots soon learned how to operate through and around the clutter so that it was no longer dangerous. It was merely a nuisance. Pilots literally learned how to separate the "wheat from the chaff"!

In life, Satan continues to devise new methods to clutter, snow, or becloud our corridors to God.

There are many among us who would spread strips of doubt along these pathways by proclaiming that there is no God, or that God is not our Father, or that He is too busy to hear or answer our prayers.

If we were to abandon, even temporarily, the airlane corridors to West Berlin, the Communists would immediately claim victory, and it is very possible that these corridors could never be opened again.

In the same way we must maintain daily flights along the corridors to our Father in heaven through our prayers if we are to find our way through the obstacles that Satan places in our way. If we pray daily with our families in faith, the clutter of doubts along the way will no longer be dangerous. We will find our way through these nuisances and maintain communication with our Father in heaven. He will give us the wisdom to lead our families.

To pass through the security guard at the airport before boarding a plane, one must walk through a simulated "mine detector" that detects any concealed metal objects we might carry. It is particularly sensitive to anything in the nature of weapons or bombs or other similar threats to aviation safety.

If metal is found on a person, there is an immediate buzz by the detector. Instantly that individual is pulled out of line and searched. He must disclose all that he is carrying.

Any person who is "clean" walks through the detector unmolested and may board his flight.

It would be interesting if we had a "spiritual" mine detector, so to speak, one that would detect any spiritual impurities in our soul. Such an instrument would help us bring our sins into the open and overcome them.

It would also be comforting to us to know that we had "passed the test" when we stepped through the device without so much as a "click" of the buzzer.

Certainly such a clean and unblemished condition would help us to establish better and less cluttered communication with our Father in heaven when we pray to Him for guidance for our families.

A young father was travelling in his station wagon with his wife and three children. As this family drove along the highway there suddenly came a severe windstorm.

As the storm increased in intensity, the father was suddenly impressed that he should stop the car and give the family the opportunity to unite in prayer. As they started up again they discovered that the next section of the highway was completely covered with debris. Some of it was heavy, metallic debris that had blown loose from an adjacent trailer court during the heavy windstorm.

Had they proceeded on their way without stopping to pray, they would have been caught in the midst of the flying debris with the very great likelihood of flying glass and metal (probably severe) injuries to members of their family.

The Lord whispers to us through His Spirit, but we must attune ourselves so that we might *hear* the whispering of His Spirit.

Another young couple was travelling toward another city where they were to meet with the stake president. They were summoned there by the stake president with the admonition that they would be asked for additional contributions to purchase some land next to the stake farm.

As they proceeded on their way they discussed the many contributions they were already making to the Church: a full tithing, welfare assessment, building fund, fast offering, and budget. This amount, in addition to the cost of driving over one hundred miles to the welfare farm to work each Saturday, had already overtaxed their limited funds.

Between them they decided they could not comply with the request by the stake president and were fully prepared to tell him so when they arrived. At the meeting the stake president proceeded to tell them that he didn't know why the Church needed the additional land, but it had been definitely revealed to him as stake president that he was to purchase this land for the Church. He had also been inspired to call these certain people to give additional contributions to make this purchase possible.

The young couple exchanged glances — knowing glances — realizing that they had already made up their minds to tell the stake president they could not accede to his request.

Then the stake president gave those present a special promise. Not only would they be blessed spiritually and temporally but they would be blessed *physically* for making this additional sacrifice.

Now the young couple exchanged knowing glances again. However, this time their thinking changed. For several years they had been praying for another child and this wish had not yet been granted.

How could they pray to their Father in heaven with the expectation of His answering their prayer when they failed to respond to His request of them for further sacrifice? This time their glances conveyed the message that they would gladly make any additional sacrifices necessary to meet the requests of their stake president.

Within a couple of months conception occurred, and their home was soon blessed with another child.

Prayer consists not only in asking for our needs, but also in expressing a sincere willingness to do whatever the Lord requests of us.

Prayer can and should play a vital role in strengthening family ties!

CHAPTER 13

Sensing Unspoken Needs

Albert Einstein's wife, it is said, was asked if she understood Einstein's Theory of Relativity. She thought for a moment, then answered, "No, I'm afraid I don't understand that theory, but I do think I understand Albert Einstein."

It wasn't necessary that Mrs. Einstein understand her husband's intricate theory of relativity, but it was important that she understand him.

Each of us has good days and bad days. Everyone has days when he or she needs special understanding. Understanding is one of the greatest needs in marriage — a type of understanding that doesn't demand great explanations or inquisitions.

Someone has said, "If you always plow a straight furrow, it may be because you are in a rut." This is probably true in marriage. If it is entirely uneventful and without any problems, it may be somewhat boring and humdrum.

The first thing a person should learn about marriage is that it has its ups and downs. It has its good days and its bad days.

Anyone who has driven along Western highways any distance at all is familiar with the odor of a skunk. The substance called mercaptan is the offending chemical found in skunk odor. It's not only pungent but it is also persistent. In fact, it's unbelievable how each car can carry so much of the odor away and yet leave plenty there for hundreds and hundreds of cars that follow after it.

But skunk odor has "staying power." In fact, some of the more expensive perfumes obtain their staying power or persistence by the small amounts of skunk odor that have been added.

One of the great differences between expensive perfume and ordinary aftershave lotion, for instance, is not only the more pleasant aroma of the expensive perfume, but the fact that it will persist for a longer time. And whereas the aroma of aftershave lotion disappears in a matter of minutes, the attractive aroma of an expensive perfume must linger for an entire evening and even longer.

This staying power is also necessary in marriage. Too many divorced couples have 20-20 vision — hindsight. Too many will admit that they could have made a go of their marriage had they been more persistent, if they had used more "staying power" when the going was a little rough.

If we can "hang in there" through the bad days, there are always better days ahead.

We should not expect our spouse to be a mind reader but we should try to be one ourselves. We should try to "read" each other's minds and try to anticipate each other's unspoken needs.

Few things tear down a woman's self-respect quicker than a parsimonious husband who is niggardly with her. She should enjoy the same trust and confidence with her finances as he allots himself. She should be as familiar with family finances and family expenditures as he.

Nor should she be deprived of an allowance similiar to his, one that allows her some independence. She should have an agreed amount that is hers to do with as she pleases, without any accounting to her husband or to others. Such amounts, however small, permit birthday surprises for others as well as for personal needs of an intimate nature. She should never have to "beg" for money from her husband.

But an even greater detriment to marriage is the rationing or ransoming of sex. Sex in marriage should never have a price tag placed upon it. To portion out sex to a partner is to degrade it to the level of a streetwalker. Sex is God-given and God-ordained and God-intended. It serves two purposes. One is to procreate and the other is to strengthen the marriage bond.

If it is to serve either of these noble purposes it must be a mutually shared and mutually enjoyable part of marriage. Generally speaking, when all else in the marriage is as it should be, sex will fall into its natural and normal place — and pace.

When sex is not mutually enjoyed and cherished, it is not because the partners need a psychiatrist. They usually need to have their relationship rather than their heads examined.

It requires insight on the part of each spouse and an uncanny sense of unspoken needs to make a successful marriage. Each should be so attuned to the other that it is seldom necessary to "ask" for sex.

In general, a man should realize that one does not take a roast out of the deep freeze and immediately place it in the oven. It must be thawed out first. A man should realize that a woman must be courted, must be adored, cherished, loved, and wooed in order to have her respond in true warmth.

In the same sense a woman must realize that it is no fun for a man to go to bed with a dead fish. She must anticipate and prepare and bring warmth to the marriage bed.

When sincere efforts on the part of both spouses fail to correct a faulty sex relationship, they should seek the help of their physician. If he is unable to help them, he can perhaps refer them to a capable marriage counselor.

It was Zsa Zsa Gabor, I think, who said: "Men are like fires. If they are left untended they tend to go out." The same could be said about women.

Each partner should try to sense and meet the needs of the other, whether this pertains to sex, money, or comfort and understanding. If each partner works hard *for* the marriage, it will usually succeed.

And certainly the sensing of unspoken needs plays an important role in strengthening family ties.

CHAPTER 14

It Is Not Enough Just to Love

Perfume may be beautiful to look at. It may even come in exotic containers that pique our senses. But perfume really serves no great purpose as long as it remains in the bottle. The cork must be removed, the aroma must be released and made available to be appreciated.

Love unexpressed is like a rosebud that is not allowed to unfold its petals. Everyone has the need to be assured and reassured, to be told and retold, over and over again of his or her worth. Such assurance is just as important to the soul as food is to the body.

Affection is to the heart what sunshine is to a flower. It is possible for a person to literally starve to death for affection. One may become too old for sex but one never becomes too old for love.

Marriage is similar to looking at railroad tracks. The farther down the tracks one looks, the closer the rails run together. The longer one is married, the closer the relationship should become. And the longer you are married the better your spouse is for *you* and the better he or she should look to you.

Success in marriage is not so much in *finding* the right person as it is in *being* the right person.

Love has a voracious appetite. It must be fed daily a well-balanced diet of affection, consideration, kindness and compassion. Someone has postulated that if we were all told we had only five minutes to live, immediately every phone in the land would be busy as we tried to contact the ones we love most to tell them how much we love them. If this love is so important, why wait until the last five minutes of life to *express* it.

Most people know what a pipe wrench is. Certainly to perform most plumbing repairs one has to have a pipe wrench. It grasps the pipe firmly with its teeth, allowing us to turn it in or out of its fittings.

I don't know when or by whom the wrench was invented. It has been around longer than I have. But I remember learning something about the pipe wrench when I was just a boy.

Because of its design, a pipe wrench works only when it is turned in the right direction. If one tries to turn it the opposite direction it simply slips off and will not do the job.

Marriage is very similar to a pipe wrench. If we want it to work we have to turn it in the right direction. Our Father in heaven, having designed marriage as the way for His children, has also given us some guidelines to follow if we are to succeed.

He has told us how to turn our marriage in the right direction to make it work. In this book we have tried to outline some of those signposts along the way.

As a man was telling me the plight of his marriage, he remarked that he and his wife did not enjoy doing anything together. Because I also knew this man as a close friend I began to recount some of the good times I remembered in their life.

As we reminisced he recalled with considerable joy many of these good times they had experienced. With some embarrassment he then recalled the statement he had made at the beginning of the conversation.

"But that was then," he said. "It isn't that way now."

"Perhaps you have forgotten the good times you once had together," I said. "It would be interesting if every couple were required to keep a diary of the good times, the joys, and the triumphs in their lives. If recorded so that it reflected the ecstasy of the moment, it would be an eye-opener for some of you who seem to have forgotten.

"If a judge were then to open such a diary in the divorce courtroom and read of these experiences to the contending couple, it might set to naught their premise of having nothing in common, and no common interests."

Too often we blow up small differences into gigantic bubbles, all out of proportion, forgetting the great memories we share and treasure. We forget all the priceless moments we have experienced together. Consider, for instance, the advent of the first child. Recall the illnesses through which we have kept a constant vigil together, and the relief we experienced when the crisis was over.

Recall the times we knelt arm in arm in prayer as we faced a crisis. Recount the faith we felt and the love of the Lord we shared.

In some instances divorce is not only necessary, but it may be a blessing. But in certain other cases couples merely exchange one set of problems for another. They will probably find it easier to repair and rebuild their present marriage than to launch into another relationship with only the *hope* that it might be better than the present one.

The old Christian hymn counselled us to "count your many blessings, see what God has done." As far as our marriage is concerned, perhaps we might do the same thing and *express* our love and our gratitude for each other.

Let's polish up the silver and see if the old luster isn't still there. It may just be hidden from view by the tarnish of neglect. The love is still there underneath, strong as ever. It merely needs to find more frequent expression.

While visiting a resort in California my wife and I watched a blacksmith fashion a miniature horseshoe.

He had a primitive blacksmith shop with all the original smithy's tools. There was a hand bellows with which he fired the coal into a white-hot bed as he turned and carefully arranged the clinkers to receive the steel.

His anvil rang with the familiar sound that I recalled from my own boyhood as I watched our own small-town blacksmith repair wagons and shoe horses. Typically, he struck a blow on the hot steel, then a ringing blow on the anvil almost as if he were pounding out the "Anvil Chorus".

Children and adults stood enchanted as the long, round, crude bar of steel was poked into the fire. Quickly it became white hot, and was withdrawn and slowly fashioned, flattened, pounded and shaped.

Then it was reinserted into the fire, and the entire process repeated again and again until the final product emerged as a well-shaped horseshoe.

As the blacksmith held it up from time to time to examine it from all angles to see if it met with his standards, one could tell that he was really proud of his product.

It was a work of art, this horseshoe.

To city dwellers, and especially to children who have never seen a blacksmith or his shop, all of this was fascinating.

But what we also remember is one statement that the blacksmith repeated every time he plunged the steel into the fire and pumped the bellows:

"Remember, steel is no good for forging unless it is hot!"

It is difficult to change a marriage whose love has grown lukewarm or even cold from boredom. But just as the blacksmith pumped his hand bellows to turn smoldering coals into a white-hot flame, we can rejuvenate our marriage and fan the flames of love once more.

Marriage is not a car that runs without power. Nor does it steer itself like a train on a track. We must work at it, stoke the fire in the boilers, change the switches to take us where we want to go — and travel along together.

The sights and experiences we have along the way will

be worth it, especially when travelling with the someone we love.

Someone has said: "It is important to marry the one you love but it is more important to love the one you marry."

In any event, the happiness and the success of that marriage will depend upon whether that love is expressed or not. Only when it is expressed will it strengthen family ties.